Student Activities Manual

Student Activities Manual

EXPLORACIONES

SECOND EDITION

Mary Ann Blitt
College of Charleston

Margarita Casas
Linn-Benton Community College

CENGAGE
Learning·

Australia • Brazil • Japan • Korea • Mexico • Singapore • Spain • United Kingdom • United States

Exploraciones Second Edition
Student Activities Manual
Blitt | Casas

© 2016 Cengage Learning®

WCN: 01-100-101

For product information and technology assistance, contact us at
Cengage Learning Customer & Sales Support, 1-800-354-9706.

For permission to use material from this text or product, submit all requests online at **www.cengage.com/permissions.**
Further permissions questions can be e-mailed to
permissionrequest@cengage.com.

ISBN: 978-1-305-25773-3

Cengage Learning
20 Channel Center Street
Boston, MA 02210
USA

Cengage Learning is a leading provider of customized learning solutions with office locations around the globe, including Singapore, the United Kingdom, Australia, Mexico, Brazil, and Japan. Locate your local office at **www.cengage.com/global.**

Cengage Learning products are represented in Canada by Nelson Education, Ltd.

To learn more about Cengage Learning Solutions, visit **www.cengage.com.**

Purchase any of our products at your local college store or at our preferred online store **www.cengagebrain.com.**

Printed in the United States of America
Print Number: 02   Print Year: 2015

CONTENIDO

CAPÍTULO 1 Hola, ¿qué tal?

Prueba tu vocabulario 1

1.1 **Saludos** Complete the following conversations with an appropriate word from the vocabulary.

Conversación 1:

SUSANA: ¡(1.) _____, Rafael!

RAFAEL: Hola, Susana. ¿(2.) _____

(3.) _____ tú?

SUSANA: Bien. ¿Y (4.) _____?

RAFAEL: Muy bien. Susana, te

(5.) _____ a mi amigo, Ronaldo.

SUSANA: Mucho gusto. ¿(6.) De _____

(7.) _____?

RONALDO: Soy (8.) _____ Puerto Rico.

RAFAEL: Bueno, adiós, Susana.

SUSANA: (9.) _____.

Conversación 2:

ESTUDIANTE: (1.) _____

(2.) _____, señor.

PROFESOR: Hola. ¿Cómo estás?

ESTUDIANTE: Bien, gracias. ¿Y

(3.) _____?

PROFESOR: Muy bien gracias. ¿Cómo

(4.) _____ llamas?

ESTUDIANTE: (5.) _____

(6.) _____ José Luis.

PROFESOR: Yo soy el señor Gómez.

ESTUDIANTE: Mucho (7.) _____.

1.2 **El salón de clase** Write the vocabulary word for the items numbered in the picture below. Do not forget to include the article: **el, la, los,** or **las.**

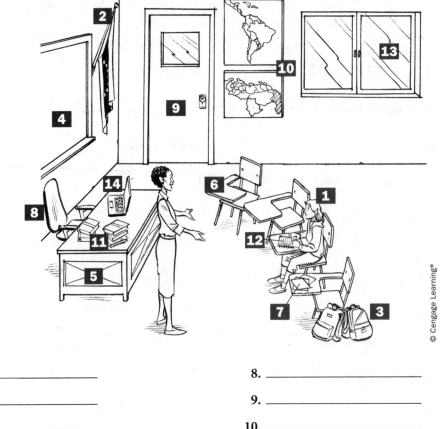

1. _____
2. _____
3. _____
4. _____
5. _____
6. _____
7. _____

8. _____
9. _____
10. _____
11. _____
12. _____
13. _____
14. _____

1.3 **Palabras escondidas** Unscramble the letters to form words from the chapter's vocabulary.

1. boilr _____

2. oiicdorcani _____

3. terpuip _____

4. dranaeb _____

5. daconuer _____

6. jrloe _____

7. avennat _____

8. zliáp _____

Prueba tu gramática 1 y 2

Gender and number of nouns

1.4 **En mi clase** Complete the following paragraph with the plural form of the vocabulary words in parentheses.

En mi clase hay veinte (1.) _____ (estudiante), dos (2.) _____ (profesor), cuatro (3.) _____ (ventana), dos (4.) _____ (televisor), tres (5.) _____ (pizarra), cuatro (6.) _____ (cartel) y muchos (7.) _____ (pupitre). En mi mochila hay cinco (8.) _____ (libro), tres (9.) _____ (cuaderno), dos (10.) _____ (lápiz) y muchos (11.) _____ (papel).

1.5 **¿Masculino o femenino?** Look at the following list of vocabulary words and decide whether they are masculine or feminine. Write **M** in the blank in front of the word if it is masculine and **F** if it is feminine.

1. _____ bandera
2. _____ bolígrafo
3. _____ escritorio
4. _____ silla

5. _____ pupitre
6. _____ reloj
7. _____ profesor
8. _____ mapa

9. _____ computadora
10. _____ cartel
11. _____ puerta
12. _____ lápiz

1.6 **¿Cuántos hay?** Write out the numbers in parentheses.

En el salón de clases hay...

1. (20) _____ pupitres
2. (3) _____ mapas
3. (11) _____ bolígrafos
4. (18) _____ estudiantes
5. (9) _____ diccionarios

6. (5) _____ ventanas
7. (14) _____ libros
8. (4) _____ sillas
9. (7) _____ carteles
10. (15) _____ mochilas

1.7 **Una secuencia lógica** Write the number that logically completes each sequence.

1. dos, cuatro, seis, ocho, _____, doce, _____, _____, dieciocho, _____

2. tres, seis, _____, doce, _____, _____

3. cinco, diez, _____, _____

4. cuatro, ocho, _____, dieciséis, _____

5. veinte, diecisiete, catorce, _____, _____, cinco, _____

Definite and indefinite articles and **hay**

1.8 **Los artículos** Change the definite articles to indefinite articles.

Modelo la pizarra   Hay __*una*__ pizarra.

1. el libro   Hay _____ libro.

2. los mapas   Hay _____ mapas.

3. la estudiante   Hay _____ estudiante.

4. las sillas   Hay _____ sillas.

5. los lápices   Hay _____ lápices.

6. la puerta   Hay _____ puerta.

7. las mochilas   Hay _____ mochilas.

8. el escritorio   Hay _____ escritorio.

1.9 **El salón de clase** Complete the following paragraph with the correct definite and indefinite articles.

Esta *(This)* es (1.) _____ clase de geografía y el señor Díaz es (2.) _____ profesor de la

clase. (3.) _____ salón de clases está muy organizado. Hay (4.) _____ escritorio enfrente

(to the front) de la clase y hay (5.) _____ pizarra entre *(between)* (6.) _____ puerta y

(7.) _____ ventana. Hay (8.) _____ pupitres y (9.) _____ libros en los pupitres.

Hay (10.) _____ mapa en la clase. (11.) _____ mapa es muy grande.

1.10 **En la mochila** Look at the picture below and answer the questions in complete sentences, using the verb form **hay.**

> **Modelo** ¿Cuántas mochilas hay? *Hay una mochila.*

© Cengage Learning®

1. ¿Cuántos bolígrafos hay? _____

2. ¿Cuántos cuadernos hay? _____

3. ¿Cuántos libros hay? _____

4. ¿Cuántas computadoras hay? _____

5. ¿Cuántos lápices hay? _____

6. ¿Cuántos papeles hay? _____

1.11 **Los números de teléfono** Spell out the following telephone numbers. Remember to use double digits whenever possible!

> **Modelo** 5-10-11-42 *cinco, diez, once, cuarenta y dos*

1. 9-87-65-43 _____

2. 4-12-34-56 _____

3. 3-71-22-19 _____

4. 2-14-98-15 _____

5. 8-67-53-09 _____

¡Hora de escuchar! 1

🔊 **1.12** **Saludos** Listen to a conversation between friends and fill in the missing words.
1-2

ÓSCAR: (1.) ¡ _____ ! ¿Cómo estás?

NORMA: ¡Hola, Óscar! Estoy (2.) _____, ¿y tú?

ÓSCAR: (3.) _____. Hay un examen en (4.) _____ de español.

NORMA: Óscar, te (5.) _____ a mi amiga, Reina.

ÓSCAR: (6.) _____. ¿Qué tal?

REINA: Bien, (7.) _____.

ÓSCAR: Bueno, mucho gusto y (8.) _____.

NORMA y REINA: (9.) _____.

🔊 **1.13** **En la clase** Look at the three pictures below and then listen to the statements. Decide to which
1-3   drawing each statement refers.

A.   **B.**   **C.**

© Cengage Learning®

1. _____   2. _____   3. _____   4. _____   5. _____   6. _____

🔊 **1.14** **¿Cierto o falso?** Listen to Lorenzo's description of his classroom and decide whether the
1-4   following statements are true (**cierto**) or false (**falso**). Rewrite any false statements to make them true.

1. Cierto Falso   Hay 20 estudiantes en la clase de español.

_____

2. Cierto Falso   Hay mapas en la clase.

_____

3. Cierto Falso   Hay una bandera en la clase.

_____

4. Cierto Falso   Hay un bolígrafo en el escritorio.

_____

5. Cierto Falso   Hay pupitres para (*for*) los estudiantes.

_____

Pronunciación 1: El alfabeto

🔊 Listen to the pronunciation of the letters of the alphabet and the first names and repeat during the pause.
1-5

A	a	Ana	Andrés
B	be	Bárbara	Boris
C	ce	Cecilia	Carlos
D	de	Dora	David
E	e	Eva	Edgar
F	efe	Fátima	Federico
G	ge	Graciela	Gilberto
H	hache	Hilda	Héctor
I	i	Inés	Ignacio
J	jota	Julia	Jacinto
K	ka	Karina	Kaitán
L	ele	Lola	Lucas
M	eme	Marisela	Manolo
N	ene	Norma	Néstor
Ñ	eñe	Begoña	Íñigo
O	o	Olivia	Óscar
P	pe	Patricia	Pablo
Q	cu	Quirina	Quinto
R	ere	Ariana	Rafael
S	ese	Sara	Salvador
T	te	Teresa	Tomás
U	u	Úrsula	Ulises
V	uve	Vanesa	Víctor
W	doble uve	Winifreda	Walter
X	equis	Xochitl	Xavier
Y	ye	Yolanda	Yamil
Z	zeta	Zoraida	Zacarías

🔊 **A.** Listen to the spelling of six Spanish words and write them in the spaces below.
1-6

1. _____   4. _____

2. _____   5. _____

3. _____   6. _____

B. Using what you have learned about cognates, tell what the words above mean.

1. _____   4. _____

2. _____   5. _____

3. _____   6. _____

¡Hora de escribir!

It is the first day of school and these students are meeting for the first time. Write a dialogue between two of the students.

Paso 1 List a variety of ways you could greet your classmates.

Paso 2 What expression would you use to introduce yourself? How might the other person introduce himself/herself? What expressions would be appropriate responses to an introduction?

Paso 3 List a variety of ways you might ask how someone is doing. Then jot down a variety of ways you might respond to a question about how you are doing.

Paso 4 List a variety of ways you might say goodbye to someone.

© Yuri Arcurs/Shutterstock

Paso 5 Using the expressions you came up with in **Pasos 1–4,** write a dialogue between two of the students in which you include a greeting, an introduction, how someone is feeling, and a farewell.

Paso 6 Edit your dialogue:

1. Were you consistent in using the informal all the way through the dialogue?

2. Check your spelling, including accent marks.

_____

_____

_____

_____

_____

_____

_____

_____

_____

_____

_____

_____

_____

Prueba tu vocabulario 2

1.15 Los antónimos Write the vocabulary word that means the opposite of the one given.

1. difícil _____

2. antipático _____

3. cruel _____

4. bueno _____

5. trabajador _____

6. generoso _____

7. paciente _____

8. interesante _____

9. realista _____

10. optimista _____

1.16 ¿El chico o el perro? Decide whether the following words describe the boy or his dog, and write the corresponding letter.

© Cengage Learning®

a. el chico   b. el perro

1. _____ alto

2. _____ agresivo

3. _____ antipático

4. _____ delgado

5. _____ feo

6. _____ gordo

7. _____ joven

8. _____ moreno

9. _____ simpático

1.17 Asociaciones Write the most logical adjective to describe each person or thing.

Modelo el salón de clases: _grande_ grande cruel

1. el presidente _____   idealista   corto

2. un libro _____   largo   pobre

3. Antonio Banderas _____   trabajador   fácil

4. un estudiante _____   largo   alto

5. un reloj _____   nuevo   guapo

6. un cuaderno _____   simpático   bueno

Prueba tu gramática 3 y 4

Subject pronouns and the verb ser

1.18 Grupos The following pronouns are singular, indicating that they refer to only one person. What pronoun(s) would you use to make each term refer to more than one person? Be sure to list all possible pronouns for each item.

Modelo él *ellos*

1. ella _____

2. yo _____

3. tú _____

4. usted _____

1.19 Los pronombres Replace each name with the appropriate pronoun.

Modelo Juan *él*

1. Marcela _____

2. Jorge y Carlos _____

3. Leo y yo _____

4. Cecilia y tú _____

5. Susanita *(when speaking **to** her)* _____

6. Gilberto _____

7. Roberto y Eva _____

8. la señora Gómez *(when speaking **to** her)* _____

1.20 El verbo ser Complete the following chart with the correct forms of the verb **ser.**

yo	_____	nosotros(as)	_____
tú	_____	vosotros(as)	_____
él	_____	ellos	_____
ella	_____	ellas	_____
usted	_____	ustedes	_____

1.21 ¿Quién? Read each sentence and circle the appropriate subject pronoun.

Modelo (Mariana / Yo) es guapa.

1. (Nosotros / Ellas) somos inteligentes.

2. (Tú / Usted) eres simpático.

3. (Vosotros / Ustedes) sois estudiantes.

4. (Tú / Usted) es un profesor estricto.

5. (Ustedes / Vosotros) son rubios.

6. (Ella / Yo) es de México.

1.22 **¿De dónde eres tú?** Complete the following paragraph with the correct forms of the verb **ser.**

Mi amigo y yo (1.) _____ de Venezuela. Yo (2.) _____ de Caracas, y él (3.) _____ de

Maracaibo. Nuestras novias (*Our girlfriends*) se llaman Gisela y Elena. Ellas (4.) _____ de Colombia.

Gisela (5.) _____ de Bogotá y Elena (6.) _____ de Medellín. ¿De dónde (7.) _____ tú?

Adjective agreement

1.23 **¿A quién describe?** Next to each adjective, write in the letter or letters that correspond to everyone it could describe. **¡OJO!** Many of the adjectives can be used with more than one subject. Pay attention to gender and number!

Modelo _____ perezosos __*d, e*__

a. Gloria   b. Miguel   c. Gloria y Beatriz   d. Miguel y Óscar   e. Gloria y Miguel

1. _____ atlético
2. _____ cariñosa
3. _____ cómico
4. _____ generosa
5. _____ honestos
6. _____ inteligente
7. _____ joven

8. _____ liberales
9. _____ optimistas
10. _____ pacientes
11. _____ serias
12. _____ simpáticos
13. _____ tímida
14. _____ trabajador

1.24 **Mis amigos** Complete the sentences by rewriting the underlined adjective so that it agrees with the subject in the second clause.

Modelo Mi amigo es <u>alto</u> y mi amiga también es *alta*.

1. Mi amigo es <u>simpático</u> y mi amiga también es _____.

2. Mi amiga es <u>seria</u> y mi amigo también es _____.

3. Mi amiga es <u>guapa</u> y mi amigo también es _____.

4. Mi amigo es <u>inteligente</u> y mis amigas también son _____.

5. Mi amigo es <u>trabajador</u> y mis amigas también son _____.

6. Mis amigos son <u>amables</u> y mis amigas también son _____.

7. Mi amiga es <u>idealista</u> y mi amigo también es _____.

8. Mi amigo es <u>honesto</u> y mi amiga también es _____.

1.25 **¿Cómo son?** Describe the people using the adjectives provided. **¡OJO!** Pay attention to adjective agreement (masculine vs feminine and singular vs plural).

1. Los profesores son _____ y _____. (paciente, serio)

2. Las estudiantes son _____ y _____. (simpático, joven)

3. Nosotros somos _____ y _____. (trabajador, tímido)

4. Mi amiga es _____ y _____. (alto, pelirrojo)

5. Mi amigo es _____ y _____. (optimista, sociable)

1.26 **Descripciones** Complete the following sentences with the correct form of the verb **ser** and two different adjectives. **¡OJO!** Pay attention to the form of the adjective!

Modelo Gael García Bernal *es guapo y delgado.*

1. Yo _____

2. Mi amigo y yo _____

3. Mi profesor(a) de español _____

4. George López y Gabriel Iglesias _____

5. Shakira y Salma Hayek _____

6. Marc Anthony y Jennifer López _____

7. Sofía Vergara _____

¡Hora de escuchar! 2

🔊 **1.27** **La fila** Listen to the statements about the people in the drawing and decide whether they are true
1-7 (**cierto**) or false (**falso**).

El Sr. González   Magdalena   Sergio   La Sra. Valdez

1. Cierto Falso   5. Cierto Falso

2. Cierto Falso   6. Cierto Falso

3. Cierto Falso   7. Cierto Falso

4. Cierto Falso   8. Cierto Falso

🔊 **1.28** **¿Quién es?** You will hear several descriptions. Look at the drawings and write the letter that
1-8 corresponds to the description you hear.

a.

b.

c.

d.

e.

© Cengage Learning®

1. _____ 2. _____ 3. _____ 4. _____ 5. _____ 6. _____ 7. _____ 8. _____

🔊 **1.29** **Respuestas lógicas** Listen to the questions or statements and choose the most appropriate
1-9 response.

1. _____   a. Antonio.   b. Bien, gracias.

2. _____   a. Nada.   b. Regular.

3. _____   a. Mucho gusto.   b. ¡Nos vemos!

4. _____   a. Soy de Perú.   b. Soy Ramón.

5. _____   a. Muy bien.   b. Nada.

Pronunciación 2: Las vocales

🔊 Unlike English, Spanish vowels are consistent in their pronunciation, regardless of the other sounds
1-10 around them.

A is pronounced like the **a** in *father.*

E is pronounced like the **a** in *cake.*

I is pronounced like the **ee** in *feel.*

O is pronounced like the **o** in *woke.*

U is pronounced like the **oo** in *tooth.*

Listen to the pronunciation of the vowels in the following rhyme.

A E I O U

El burro sabe más que tú.

🔊 Now listen and repeat the following words and their vowel sounds.
1-11

A	Ana	mañana	banana	papá
E	me	Pepe	nene	bebé
I	sí	Pili	Trini	Mimi
O	no	Toño	coco	poco
U	tú	Lulú	gurú	Zulu

¡Hora de reciclar!

1.30 **Los artículos** Complete the sentences with the correct article (**un, unos, una, unas, el, los, la, las**).

Modelo   En el salón de clases hay ___*una*___ pizarra negra.

1. _____ libro de español es interesante.

2. _____ estudiantes de la clase son simpáticas.

3. En la clase hay _____ chico de España.

4. _____ computadoras del laboratorio son nuevas.

5. _____ profesora es extrovertida.

6. En el salón de clases hay un mapa. _____ mapa es de Latinoamérica.

7. En mi mochila hay _____ diccionario.

8. _____ ventanas del salón de clases son grandes.

CAPÍTULO 2 ¿Cómo es tu vida?

Prueba tu vocabulario 1

2.1 **Los miembros de la familia** Use the clues to complete the words.

1. Es la hermana de mi padre. T __ __

2. Es la hija de mi madre y de mi padrastro. M __ __ __ A H __ __ __ __ __ A

3. Es el hijo de mi hijo. N __ __ __ O

4. Es la madre de mi esposo. S __ __ __ __ A

5. Son los hijos de mis tíos. P __ __ __ __ S

6. Son los hijos de mi hermano. S __ __ __ __ __ __ S

7. Son los padres de mis padres. A __ __ __ __ __ S

8. Es la esposa de mi padre, pero no es mi madre. M __ __ __ __ __ __ __ A

2.2 **Más sobre la familia** Use the family tree to complete the sentences below.

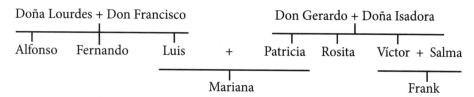

Doña Lourdes + Don Francisco   Don Gerardo + Doña Isadora

Alfonso   Fernando   Luis   +   Patricia   Rosita   Víctor + Salma

Mariana   Frank

1. Mariana es la _____ de Frank.

2. Alfonso y Fernando son _____.

3. Mariana es la _____ de doña Lourdes y doña Lourdes es la _____ de Mariana.

4. Patricia es la _____ de Frank.

5. Rosita es la _____ de don Gerardo y doña Isadora.

6. Mariana es la _____ de Fernando.

7. Don Gerardo es el _____ de Salma.

8. Todos los miembros de la familia de Patricia son los _____ de Patricia.

2.3 **¿Cierto o falso?** Read the following statements and decide if they are true (**cierto**) or false (**falso**).

1. Cierto   Falso   Mi tío es el hermano de mi papá.

_____

2. Cierto   Falso   Mi prima es la hija de mi hermana.

_____

3. Cierto   Falso   Mi abuelo es el padre de mi madre.

_____

4. Cierto   Falso   Mi tía es la madre de mi esposo.

_____

5. Cierto   Falso   Mi hermano es el hijo de mi hijo.

_____

Prueba tu gramática 1 y 2

Possessive adjectives

2.4 **La familia de Carina** Carina is talking to her friend, Gustavo, about her family. Choose the possessive adjectives that best complete the sentences.

GUSTAVO: Carina, ¿es esta una foto de (1.) _____ (tu/tus) familia?

CARINA: Sí, aquí están (2.) _____ (mi/mis) padres y ella es (3.) _____ (mi/mis) hermana, Graciela.

(4.) _____ (Nuestro/Nuestra) tía está aquí. Ella es la hermana de (5.) _____ (mi/mis) padre.

GUSTAVO: ¿Ella tiene esposo?

CARINA: Sí, pero (6.) _____ (su/sus) esposo no está en la foto. Él viaja mucho. (7.) _____ (Su/Sus) hijos no

están en la foto tampoco *(either)*. Están en la universidad.

GUSTAVO: ¿Y ustedes tienen mascotas?

CARINA: Sí, (8.) _____ (nuestros/nuestras) gatas se llaman Natasha, Tomasa y Traviesa.

2.5 **La opción correcta** Decide which form of the adjectives in parentheses is needed to complete the paragraph.

Yo tengo dos hermanas. (1.) _____ (Mi) hermanas son simpáticas. Ellas y yo tenemos muchas

mascotas. (2.) _____ (Nuestro) mascotas son pequeñas porque (3.) _____ (nuestro) casa

también es pequeña. Tenemos dos perros. (4.) _____ (Su) nombres son Huesos y Peludo. Huesos es

un perro tonto, pero él es _____ (5.) (mi) mascota favorita.

2.6 **El apartamento** Complete the following paragraph with the correct possessive adjectives.

Mi compañero y yo vivimos en un apartamento. (1.) _____ apartamento no es muy grande, pero

estamos contentos allí. (2.) _____ compañero (roommate) se llama Óscar, y él tiene unas mascotas.

(3.) _____ perro es pequeño y muy simpático, pero (4.) _____ gatos son antipáticos. Yo

tengo dos hermanas y cuando (5.) _____ hermanas vienen (come) les gusta jugar (they like to play)

con (6.) _____ animales. ¿Y tú? ¿Cómo es la vida en (7.) _____ casa?

2.7 **¿De quién es?** The Ramírez family has many pets. Rewrite the sentences using the possessive adjective **su(s)**.

    Modelo   El pájaro es de Paquito. Es *su pájaro.*

1. El caballo es del señor Ramírez. Es _____.

2. El gato es de Luisita y Sarita. Es _____.

3. Los peces son de Miguelito. Son _____.

4. El perro es de la señora Ramírez. Es _____.

5. Los ratones son de Graciela. Son _____.

6. Las mascotas son de la familia Ramírez. Son _____.

2.8 **Información adicional** Read the following statements and complete the additional information about the people using the missing possessive pronoun.

    Modelo   Jimena tiene un hermano.
               Su hermano tiene seis años.

1. Yo tomo tres clases. _____ clases son difíciles.

2. Los estudiantes viven en un apartamento. _____ apartamento es pequeño.

3. Tenemos muchos amigos. _____ amigos son de México.

4. Ustedes tienen un coche. _____ coche es viejo.

5. Usted compra tres libros. _____ libros son muy interesantes.

6. Mis hermanos y yo tenemos tres mascotas. _____ mascotas son un perro, un gato y un pez.

Regular -ar verbs

2.9 **¿Qué hacen?** Federico is discussing the activities he and his friends and family do. Complete his sentences using the words in parentheses. Be sure to conjugate the verbs correctly.

Modelo (hablar español) El profesor de español *habla español*.

1. (buscar un trabajo) Yo _____

2. (cocinar muy bien) Mi madre _____

3. (mandar muchos mensajes) Mis amigos _____

4. (escuchar música clásica) Mis abuelos _____

5. (trabajar en una oficina) Mi tía _____

6. (tomar clases de lenguas) Mis amigos y yo _____

7. (nadar) Mi hermano y yo _____

8. (desear viajar mucho) Yo _____

2.10 **¡Qué coincidencia!** Miranda and her new friend, Simón, are chatting about their activities and those of their siblings. Complete their conversation using the verbs in parentheses.

MIRANDA: Mi hermana Ana (1.) _____ (tomar/nadar) lecciones de canto (*singing*) todos los días.

SIMÓN: ¡Qué coincidencia! Yo también (2.) _____ (tomar/mirar) lecciones de canto. Además

(*Moreover*) yo (3.) _____ (llegar/bailar) muy bien.

MIRANDA: Yo no (4.) _____ (escuchar/tomar) lecciones de canto porque (5.) _____

(escuchar/estudiar) en la universidad y (6.) _____ (necesitar/practicar) estudiar mucho. Mis

hermanos Mario y Saúl (7.) _____ (regresar/estudiar) en la universidad también.

SIMÓN: Yo no (8.) _____ (estudiar/necesitar) en la universidad. (9.) _____ (Trabajar/

Esquiar) en una tienda (*store*) de música. ¿Tú (10.) _____ (escuchar/caminar) mucha música?

MIRANDA: Pues, sí. Yo (11.) _____ (llevar/escuchar) música todos los días.

2.11 **Una familia ocupada** Complete the following sentences with the appropriate form of the verb in parentheses.

Modelo Yo *estudio* (estudiar) español.

1. Mi familia _____ (viajar) mucho.

2. Mis hermanas _____ (bailar) ballet.

3. Mi hermano _____ (practicar)
   el fútbol.

4. Yo _____ (nadar).

5. Mis padres _____ (trabajar).

6. Mi padre _____ (manejar) un camión (*truck*).

7. Mi madre _____ (enseñar) inglés.

8. Mis hermanos y yo _____ (ayudar) a limpiar
   la casa.

2.12 **Preguntas personales** Answer these questions in complete sentences.

1. ¿Miras la televisión mucho?

_____

2. ¿Bailas bien?

_____

3. ¿Dónde trabajas?

_____

4. ¿Cuántas horas estudias normalmente?

_____

5. ¿Mandas muchos mensajes?

_____

6. ¿Deseas enseñar en el futuro?

_____

¡Hora de escuchar! 1

2.13 **La familia de Luisa** Listen to Luisa's description of her family and complete the following sentences with the correct vocabulary word. **¡OJO!** Remember that you are writing what Luisa would say.

> You will hear: *Rafael es el esposo de mi madre.*
> You will write: Rafael es mi *padre.*

1. Eduardo es mi _____.

2. Daniela es mi _____.

3. Úrsula es mi _____.

4. Beatriz y Adela son mis _____.

5. Alejandro y Eva son mis _____.

6. Felipe es mi _____.

🔊 **2.14** **¿Qué hacen?** Listen to the statements. Then write the number of the statement under the picture it describes.

1-13

a. _____

b. _____

c. _____

d. _____

e. _____

f. _____

🔊 **2.15** ¿Quién? Listen to the descriptions of Gloria and Marcelo, and decide whether the following
1-14   statements refer to Gloria, Marcelo, or both (Los dos).

1. Marcelo   Gloria   Los dos   Estudia en la universidad.

2. Marcelo   Gloria   Los dos   Trabaja en un restaurante.

3. Marcelo   Gloria   Los dos   Tiene novio(a).

4. Marcelo   Gloria   Los dos   Practica fútbol.

5. Marcelo   Gloria   Los dos   Escucha música.

6. Marcelo   Gloria   Los dos   Visita a su hermano.

Pronunciación 1: Diphthongs

🔊 A diphthong is the pronunciation of two vowels in one syllable. While each vowel sound is pronounced in
1-15 Spanish, the strong vowels (a, e, o) are more fully enunciated. Listen and repeat the following words.

ai – baila Haití aire

au – Paula Austria audio

ei – veinte treinta seis

eu – Europa Eugenio feudal

ia – estudia sociable farmacia

ie – tiene diez nieto

io – armario religioso escritorio

oi – oiga boicot soy

ua – Paraguay Ecuador cuarto

ue – bueno abuelo suegro

When there are two weak vowels (i, u) together, the second vowel is more fully enunciated. Listen and repeat
the following words.

iu – viudo veintiuno **ui** – Luisa cuidado

Un trabalenguas Here is a tongue twister to practice some diphthongs.

Cuando cuentas cuentos nunca cuentas cuantos cuentos cuentas,
porque cuando cuentas cuentos nunca cuentas cuantos cuentos cuentas.

¡Hora de reciclar! 1

2.16 Los artículos Complete the sentences with the correct article (un, unos, una, unas, el, los, la, las).

Modelo   En el salón de clases hay __una__ pizarra.

1. _____ libro de español es interesante.

2. Todas _____ estudiantes de la clase son simpáticas.

3. En la clase hay _____ cartel de España.

4. _____ computadoras del laboratorio son
   nuevas pero otras son de 2009.

5. _____ profesora Zarzalejos es extrovertida.

6. En el salón de clases hay un mapa. _____
   mapa es de Latinoamérica.

7. En mi mochila hay _____ diccionario.

8. _____ tres ventanas del salón de clases son grandes.

¡Hora de escribir!

Write a paragraph about the people in one of the family photos.

Paso 1 Choose one of the photos and jot down some ideas to incorporate into your paragraph. Where is the family from? What are the names of the people in the photo and what is their relationship? What are they like?

Paso 2 Write a paragraph to describe the family in the photo using the information you generated in **Paso 1.**

Paso 3 Edit your paragraph:

1. Is your paragraph logically organized or do you skip from one idea to the next?
2. Are there any short sentences you can combine by using **y** or **pero**?
3. Are there any spelling errors?
4. Do your verbs agree with the subject?
5. Do your adjectives agree with the object/person they describe?

_____

_____

_____

_____

_____

_____

Prueba tu vocabulario 2

2.17 **Sopa de letras** Unscramble the letters to form vocabulary words. All of them are school subjects.

1. sigéln _____

2. iícqmau _____

3. aífflsooi _____

4. ragfaeoíg _____

5. itmacamtsáe _____

6. ncdraóiec _____

7. brelagá _____

8. trahsioi _____

2.18 **La universidad** Complete the sentences with the most logical place on campus from the list below. Use each place only once.

el gimnasio   la librería   la cafetería   la residencia   la biblioteca   el estadio

1. Selma busca libros y estudia en _____.

2. Luli y Leticia toman café en _____.

3. Gloria nada en _____.

4. Beto y Enrique compran cuadernos, libros y lápices en _____.

5. Miranda mira un juego *(match)* de fútbol en _____.

6. Acela toma una siesta en _____.

2.19 **¿Qué clase es?** Write the class subject that best completes each sentence.

1. Los estudiantes estudian a Sócrates, Aristóteles y Platón en la clase de _____.

2. Los estudiantes tienen clase en el gimnasio y practican deportes en la clase de _____.

3. Los estudiantes trabajan con figuras como el triángulo, el círculo y el rectángulo en la clase de _____.

4. Los estudiantes son actores en la clase de _____.

5. Los estudiantes estudian las teorías de Freud en la clase de _____.

6. Los estudiantes estudian los elementos y hacen experimentos en el laboratorio en la clase de _____.

2.20 **Profesiones** Choose a logical class from the box for each one of the following professions. You cannot repeat classes.

la biología   la economía   la ingeniería   la psicología
la criminología   la expresión oral   la literatura

1. actor: _____

2. policía: _____

3. doctor: _____

4. psiquiatra: _____

5. profesor de inglés: _____

6. hombre/mujer de negocios: _____

7. arquitecto: _____

Prueba tu gramática 3 y 4

The verb **tener**

2.21 **El verbo _tener_** Fill in the blanks with the correct forms of the verb **tener**.

yo _____   nosotros(as) _____

tú _____   vosotros(as) _____

él _____   ellos _____

ella _____   ellas _____

usted _____   ustedes _____

2.22 **Los verbos _ser_ y _tener_** Complete the paragraph with the appropriate form of each verb in parentheses.

Yo (1.) _____ (ser) Yolanda, y él (2.) _____ (ser) mi esposo Julián. Nosotros

(3.) _____ (ser) de Uruguay. Yo (4.) _____ (tener) treinta y dos años, y mi esposo

(5.) _____ (tener) cuarenta años. Nosotros (6.) _____ (tener) tres niños. Andrés y

Andrea (7.) _____ (ser) gemelos _(twins)_, y (8.) _____ (tener) siete años. Verónica

(9.) _____ (tener) cinco años. ¿Y tú? ¿Cuántos años (10.) _____ (tener)?

2.23 **Combinaciones** Combine the elements listed for each item to create logical sentences. You will need to decide which verb to use and conjugate it according to the subject.

> **Modelo** ustedes / (ser/tener) / razón
> _Ustedes tienen razón._

1. Lourdes / (ser/tener) / mucha hambre

   _____

2. Mario / (ser/tener) / tres hermanos

   _____

3. nosotros / (ser/tener) / jóvenes

   _____

4. tú / (ser/tener) / frío

   _____

5. yo / (ser/tener) / veinte años

   _____

6. ellos / (ser/tener) / estudiantes

   _____

2.24 **¿Qué tienen?** Look at the pictures and complete each sentence logically, using the appropriate **tener** expression. Be sure to conjugate the verbs correctly.

Modelo Él *tiene suerte.*

1.

2.

3.

4.

5.

6.

1. Yo _____.

2. Nosotros _____.

3. El niño _____.

4. Yo _____.

5. Ellos _____.

6. Mi esposo y yo _____.

Adjective placement

2.25 **Mis clases** Rewrite these sentences, adding the adjective in parentheses. Place the adjective in the correct position and make sure it agrees with the noun it describes.

> **Modelo** La psicología es una clase. (largo)
> *La psicología es una clase larga.*

1. Este es un semestre. (bueno) _____

2. Tengo clases. (varios) _____

3. Tengo una clase de música. (clásico) _____

4. Hay estudiantes en la clase. (simpático) _____

5. El álgebra es una clase. (fácil) _____

6. Tenemos tarea en la clase. (poco) _____

7. Necesito libros para la clase de inglés. (mucho) _____

8. En la clase tenemos exámenes. (difícil) _____

9. El señor Díaz es un profesor. (amable) _____

10. No tengo notas en mis clases. (malo) _____

2.26 **Un párrafo aburrido** Add adjectives to the following paragraph to make it more interesting. You may use some of the adjectives listed below or choose others. Be creative!

aburrido	**bonito**	**inteligente**	**interesante**	**grande**	**largo**	**mucho**
nuevo	**pequeño**	**perezoso**	**simpático**	**típico**	**varios**	**viejo**

Yo tengo una clase de español. En la sala de clase hay una ventana. También hay un mapa y carteles en la pared. Mi profesora es una mujer. Hay estudiantes en la clase. Tenemos un libro para la clase y también hacemos *(we do)* actividades en la clase. Hay exámenes en la clase.

_____

_____

_____

_____

_____

_____

2.27 **Mi universidad** Form logical sentences, using the words provided. Be sure to include one of the adjectives in parentheses. **¡OJO!** Remember that the adjective must agree with the noun it describes.

Modelo   tú / tener / amigos (mucho/poco)
Tú tienes muchos amigos.

1. yo / ser / estudiante / en una universidad (público/privado)

_____

2. yo / tener / profesores (interesante/aburrido)

_____

3. mis compañeros de clase / ser / estudiantes (trabajador/perezoso)

_____

4. el español / ser / una clase (fácil/difícil)

_____

5. nosotros / tener / tarea para la clase de español (mucho/poco)

_____

_____

2.28 **¿Qué tienes?** Answer the following questions about the items you have. For each positive answer, include an adjective that describes the item. **¡OJO!** Pay attention to the form of the adjective as well as to its placement.

Modelo   ¿Tienes un apartamento?   *Sí, tengo un apartamento pequeño.*

1. ¿Tienes un auto? _____.

2. ¿Tienes amigos? _____.

3. ¿Tienes un libro? _____.

4. ¿Tienes una profesora? _____.

5. ¿Tienes una clase? _____.

¡Hora de escuchar! 2

2.29 **¿Qué clases tomas?** You will hear Tomás and Mercedes talking about all the classes they are taking this term. Write an **M** by the classes Mercedes takes and a **T** by the classes Tomás takes.

1-16

_____ química   _____ filosofía

_____ inglés   _____ teatro

_____ alemán   _____ biología

_____ álgebra   _____ informática

_____ literatura   _____ periodismo

◀))) **2.30** **¿A quién se refiere?** Listen to the conversation between Elisa and Juan and choose the correct
1-17 answers to the questions below.

1. ¿Quién tiene una clase de biología?   a. Elisa   b. Juan

2. ¿Quién tiene una clase de lenguas?   a. Elisa   b. Juan

3. ¿Quién tiene un profesor aburrido?   a. Elisa   b. Juan

4. ¿Quién tiene prisa?   a. Elisa   b. Juan

◀))) **2.31** **Descripciones** Listen to each description and write the class in Spanish that is being described.
1-18

1. _____

2. _____

3. _____

4. _____

5. _____

Pronunciación 2: La acentuación

◀))) In Spanish, for words that end in a vowel or the consonants **s** or **n,** the stress, or emphasis, is on the second-to-
1-19 last syllable. Listen to the pronunciation of the following words.

   <u>ha</u>blan   <u>co</u>rre   fe<u>bre</u>ro   be<u>be</u>mos   prima<u>ve</u>ra

If a word ends in any consonant other than **s** or **n,** the stress is on the last syllable. Listen to the pronunciation
of the following words.

   a<u>bril</u>   traba<u>jar</u>   hospi<u>tal</u>   profe<u>sor</u>   ac<u>triz</u>

In order to stress a syllable that is ordinarily not stressed, an accent mark must be used. Look at the following
words. Where would the stress normally fall? Now listen to their pronunciation.

   lápiz   exámenes   Bogotá   simpático   sillón

Accent marks are also used to distinguish one word from another.

   sí *yes*   si *if*   él *he*   el *the*

◀))) Pronounce the following words, paying particular attention to where the stress falls.
1-20

1. ideal   6. Cádiz

2. lámpara   7. teléfono

3. trabajo   8. Ecuador

4. sofá   9. escuchamos

5. farmacia

Nombre _____ Fecha _____

🔊 Now look at the following words and determine where the stress should fall. Then, listen to their
1-21 pronunciation and write accents on the letters that should have them.

1. jovenes   6. politico

2. refrigerador   7. interes

3. preocupado   8. basquetbol

4. practico   9. elefante

5. especial   10. sueter

¡Hora de reciclar! 2

2.32 **Los adjetivos** Rewrite the sentences using the new subjects provided. Remember to make sure the adjective agrees with the word it modifies and to use the appropriate form of the verb **ser**. Follow the model.

Modelo Las ciencias políticas son fáciles. El español   *es fácil.*

1. La química es difícil. Las matemáticas _____.

2. La profesora de inglés es optimista. El profesor de arte _____.

3. El libro de francés es largo. Los exámenes _____.

4. Las ciencias son interesantes. La historia _____.

5. El teatro es aburrido. La filosofía _____.

6. El examen de arte es fácil. Los exámenes de anatomía _____.

7. Los profesores de lenguas son jóvenes. La profesora de ciencias _____

_____.

8. Los estudiantes en la clase de música son trabajadores. La profesora de música _____

_____.

Capítulo 2   29

© 2016 Cengage Learning®. May not be scanned, copied or duplicated, or posted to a publicly accessible website, in whole or in part.

CAPÍTULO 3   ¿Qué tiempo hace hoy?

Prueba tu vocabulario 1

3.1 **¿Qué ropa llevan?** Write the names of the numbered items. Include the indefinite articles.

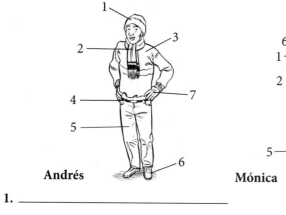

Andrés

© Cengage Learning®

Mónica

1. _____   _____

2. _____   _____

3. _____   _____

4. _____   _____

5. _____   _____

6. _____   _____

7. _____   _____

3.2 **¿Qué ropa debo llevar?** Read the weather descriptions and complete the sentences to indicate which of the listed items you would need in each case.

1. Hace mucho calor. Llevo _____.   guantes   sandalias   una bufanda

2. Llueve. Llevo _____.   una falda   calcetines   un paraguas

3. Hace frío. Llevo _____.   un abrigo   tenis   una corbata

4. Nieva. Llevo _____.   lentes   botas   una pijama

5. Hace fresco. Llevo _____.   pantalones cortos   un vestido   un suéter

6. Hace sol. Llevo _____.   un sombrero   una blusa   una bolsa

3.3 **¿Qué tiempo hace?** Describe the weather in each of the illustrations.

1. _____   2. _____   3. _____

4. _____   5. _____

3.4 **Oraciones deshidratadas** Use the words to create full sentences. **¡OJO!** You will need to add articles where appropriate.

> **Modelo** Hoy / nevar / yo / llevar / gorro →
> *Hoy nieva y yo llevo un gorro.*

1. Hoy / llover / María Inés / llevar / paraguas

2. Esta *(This)* mañana / nevar / estudiantes / llevar / abrigos

3. Esta noche / viento / profesor / llevar / impermeable

4. Hoy / despejado / tú / llevar / lentes de sol

Prueba tu gramática 1 y 2

The verb **gustar**

3.5 **¿Qué te gusta?** José Luis is writing an email to get to know a new friend better. Help him complete the email by circling the correct form of **gustar.**

¡Hola! ¿Cómo estás? ¿Te (1. gusta / gustan) el fútbol? A mí me (2. gusta / gustan) mucho todos los deportes *(sports)*; me (3. gusta / gustan) especialmente jugar al tenis y al fútbol. Pero me (4. gusta / gustan) muchas otras actividades también. Cuando no tengo clase me (5. gusta / gustan) tomar café con mis amigos. Me (6. gusta / gustan) cocinar y estudiar con mis amigos. ¿A ti te (7. gusta / gustan) cocinar? ¿Te (8. gusta / gustan) tus clases en la universidad? ¡Escribe pronto!

Nombre _____ Fecha _____

3.6 **Julio y César** Julio and his friend César have a lot in common; however they don't always like the same things. Complete the sentences telling what Julio and César like and don't like.

1. A Julio _____ tomar café, pero a César no _____ el café.

2. A Julio _____ las clases de ciencias, pero a César no _____ su clase de biología.

3. A Julio y a César _____ las novelas de ciencia ficción.

4. A Julio y a César _____ nadar y esquiar.

5. A Julio y a César _____ los animales, pero a César _____ los perros y a Julio _____ los gatos.

6. A Julio y a César _____ practicar deportes, pero a Julio _____ el fútbol y a César _____ el béisbol y el básquetbol.

3.7 **Tus gustos** Using complete sentences, express your feelings about the following things. For the last item you may choose whatever you like.

  Modelo la música en español
  Me gusta (mucho) la música en español.

1. la universidad _____

2. estudiar español _____

3. las matemáticas _____

4. las clases de ciencias _____

5. hablar en clase _____

6. ¿? _____

3.8 **Mi familia** Rodolfo is talking about his family and himself. Read his statements and complete his thoughts to indicate whether or not each person likes the item in parentheses.

  Modelo Mi hermana es estudiante de lenguas. (las clases de francés y alemán)
  Le gustan las clases de francés y alemán.

1. Yo siempre *(always)* llevo ropa muy cómoda. (las corbatas) _____

2. Mi hermano practica deportes. (el fútbol y el béisbol) _____

3. Mis tíos siempre toman vacaciones. (viajar) _____

4. Mi madre enseña matemáticas. (ayudar a los estudiantes) _____

5. Mi padre es alérgico a los animales. (los perros) _____

6. Yo soy perezoso. (cocinar y limpiar la casa) _____

Regular -er and -ir verbs

3.9 **Los fines de semana** Every weekend Mariana has exactly the same routine, with lots of activities. Look at her agenda and describe what she does. Remember to give the time for each activity.

Modelo *A las siete de la mañana Mariana recibe el periódico.*

sábado	
7:00 a.m.	recibir el periódico *(newspaper)*
10:30 a.m.	aprender a cocinar
2:15 p.m.	comer con mamá
6:50 p.m.	escribir mensajes electrónicos
9:00 p.m.	asistir al teatro

domingo	
6:30 a.m.	beber café con Tomás
8:40 a.m.	correr con amigas en el parque
9:45 p.m.	leer para la clase de inglés

© Cengage Learning®

El sábado:

1. _____

2. _____

3. _____

4. _____

El domingo:

1. _____

2. _____

3. _____

3.10 **Unas preguntas** Answer the questions in complete sentences.

1. ¿Viven tus padres en una casa o en un apartamento?

_____

2. ¿Beben café por la mañana tus amigos y tú?

_____

3. ¿Qué libros lees?

_____

4. ¿Asistes a una clase de matemáticas este semestre? ¿A qué clase?

_____

5. ¿Cuándo escribes mensajes electrónicos?

_____

3.11 **Las similitudes** Paolo is talking about activities that he has in common with his friends. Complete his description with the correct form of the verb in parentheses.

Mis amigos (1.) _____ (creer) que yo soy muy inteligente. ¡Yo también (2.) _____

(creer) que soy muy inteligente! Ellos (3.) _____ (aprender) a hablar español en la escuela;

yo también (4.) _____ (aprender) a hablar español. Mis amigos no (5.) _____

(comprender) alemán, pero yo sí (6.) _____ (comprender) un poco de alemán. Todos nosotros

(7.) _____ (vivir) en una ciudad (city) muy bonita y (8.) _____ (asistir) a la

universidad. Yo (9.) _____ (leer) mucho en mi tiempo libre y siempre (10.) _____

(recibir) muy buenas notas. Mis amigos también (11.) _____ (leer) mucho, pero ellos no

(12.) _____ (recibir) buenas notas.

3.12 **Un nuevo amigo** You met a new friend online and he has sent you some information about himself. Complete his sentences using the verbs in parentheses. Then answer his questions about yourself.

Modelo Yo __como__ (comer) muchos chocolates, ¿y tú?
(No) Como muchos chocolates.

1. Mi familia _____ (vivir) en California. ¿Vives en California?

_____

2. Mis padres _____ (comprender) español. ¿Comprendes español?

_____

3. Yo _____ (asistir) a clases de literatura. ¿Asistes a clases de literatura?

_____

4. Mis compañeros y yo _____ (leer) novelas para clase. ¿Lees novelas para clase?

_____

5. Nosotros _____ (recibir) buenas notas. ¿Recibes buenas notas?

_____

¡Hora de escuchar! 1

🔊 **3.13** **El pronóstico del tiempo** You will hear the weather forecast for several cities or regions in
1-22   Argentina. Listen carefully and answer the questions in complete sentences.

1. ¿Qué tiempo hace en Buenos Aires? _____

2. ¿Llueve en Mendoza? _____

3. ¿Qué tiempo hace en Córdoba? _____

4. ¿Cuál es la temperatura máxima en Rosario? _____

5. ¿Qué tiempo hace en la región de la Patagonia? _____

🔊 **3.14** **¿Lógico o ilógico?** You will hear six sentences about the likes and dislikes of different people.
1-23   Indicate whether the statements are logical (**lógico**) or illogical (**ilógico**).

   Modelo   You will hear: *Al chef no le gusta cocinar.*
          You will write: lógico (ilógico)

1. lógico   ilógico   4. lógico   ilógico

2. lógico   ilógico   5. lógico   ilógico

3. lógico   ilógico   6. lógico   ilógico

🔊 **3.15** **De viaje** Pepe is planning to visit Federico in Guatemala and they are having a telephone
1-24   conversation to plan the trip. Listen to their conversation and decide which of the following ideas
       complete the statements.

1. Pepe llama para preguntar...
   a. cuánto dinero debe llevar.
   b. qué tiempo hace.
   c. cómo está su amigo Federico.

2. En las montañas de Guatemala...
   a. hace mucho frío.
   b. hace mucho viento.
   c. nieva.

3. Pepe necesita llevar...
   a. un impermeable.
   b. tenis.
   c. suéteres.

4. Federico le recomienda a Pepe comprar...
   a. un paraguas para la lluvia.
   b. corbatas.
   c. suéteres en el mercado.

5. Los suéteres en el mercado...
   a. cuestan poco dinero.
   b. cuestan mucho dinero.
   c. son muy bonitos.

Pronunciación 1: Algunas consonantes

La ñ

🔊 The **ñ** is pronounced like the *ny* in English. Listen to the pronunciation of the following words.
1-25

España   Íñigo   niño   Begoña   años   cuñado   cañón   baño

La h

In Spanish, the **h** is silent except in foreign words, such as *hot dog* and *hockey.* Listen to the pronunciation of the following words.

hotel   historia   hospital   Hugo   hola   hablar   honesto

Linking

In Spanish, native speakers will link, or run together, words in the following circumstances:

1. when one word ends with the same sound the next one begins with

el libro   la antropología   las sillas   un niño

2. when one word ends with a vowel and the next begins with a vowel sound

la hamburguesa   la estudiante   cuatro horas   tú usas

3. when one word ends with a consonant and the next begins with a vowel sound

el alemán   un elefante   los estudiantes   los hospitales

🔊 Look at the following sentences and draw the link between the appropriate words. Then listen to the pronunciation
1-26 to check your answers.

1. Los hoteles son elegantes.   **4.** Los estudiantes son muy inteligentes.

2. Ella asiste a la clase de economía ahora.   **5.** La abuela tiene muchas sillas.

3. Ella es una mujer honesta.

¡Hora de reciclar! 1

3.16 **La posición de los adjetivos** Rewrite the following sentences logically, adding an appropriate
adjective from the list below. Be sure to make the adjective agree with the noun it describes. Use each
adjective only once.

calvo   corto   grande   impaciente   mucho   varios

Modelo   Tengo dos mochilas. [blanco]   *Tengo dos mochilas blancas.*

1. México tiene una universidad. _____

2. Tenemos sed. _____

3. Valentina es una niña. _____

4. Tengo un examen de cinco minutos. _____

5. Ramón tiene cursos de matemáticas: cálculo, álgebra y geometría.

_____

6. Hay dos profesores en el departamento de lenguas.

_____

¡Hora de escribir!

Write about the weather.

Paso 1 Choose one of the photos. Jot down some ideas to incorporate into your paragraph. Think about the following: What is the season? What is the date? What is the weather like? Who is the person in the photo? What is he/she doing? What is he/she wearing?

Paso 2 Write a paragraph to describe the photo you chose using the information you generated in **Paso 1.**

Paso 3 Edit your paragraph:

1. Is your paragraph logically organized or do you skip from one idea to the next?

2. Are there any short sentences you can combine by using **y** or **pero**?

3. Are there any spelling errors?

4. Do verbs agree with the subject?

© Hasloo Group Production Studio/ Shutterstock

© Maridav/Shutterstock

_____

_____

_____

_____

Prueba tu vocabulario 2

3.17 **Sopa de letras** Unscramble the letters to form the days of the week or the months of the year.

1. uvjsee _____

2. ibcerimed _____

3. tasoog _____

4. lairb _____

5. adosbá _____

6. solreméci _____

3.18 **Los meses y los días de la semana** Answer the following questions.

1. ¿Qué mes es…?
   a. el mes cuando se celebra el Día de Acción de Dar Gracias _____
   b. el mes cuando celebramos el Día de la Madre _____
   c. el último *(last)* mes del año _____
   d. el mes cuando celebramos el Día del Padre _____

2. ¿Cuál es la fecha de…?
   a. la Independencia de los Estados Unidos _____
   b. el primer día del año _____
   c. Navidad *(Christmas)* _____
   d. el Día de San Valentín _____

3.19 **La hora** Write the time for each item.

   Modelo   10:20 A.M.   *Son las diez y veinte de la mañana.*

1. 8:15 A.M. _____

2. 7:22 P.M. _____

3. 12:00 A.M. _____

4. 1:10 P.M. _____

5. 5:09 A.M. _____

6. 4:30 P.M. _____

7. 1:50 A.M. _____

8. 11:45 P.M. _____

Prueba tu gramática 3 y 4

The verb ir

3.20 **El verbo *ir*** Complete the chart with the correct forms of the verb **ir**.

yo _____   nosotros(as) _____

tú _____   vosotros(as) _____

él _____   ellos _____

ella _____   ellas _____

usted _____   ustedes _____

3.21 **En la universidad** Complete the following paragraph with the appropriate forms of the verb **ir**.

Después de *(After)* la clase de historia yo (1.) _____ a la cafetería para tomar un café con mis

amigos Ignacio y Gilberto. A las diez Ignacio y yo (2.) _____ a clase de inglés y Gilberto

(3.) _____ a clase de literatura. Al final de la clase yo (4.) _____ a la biblioteca para

estudiar e Ignacio y Gilberto (5.) _____ al gimnasio. ¿Adónde (6.) _____ tú después

de las clases?

3.22 **¿Adónde vas?** Tell where you and your friends go by completing the sentences with the correct form of the verb **ir** and the place indicated in parentheses.

    Modelo   Los viernes tú *vas al laboratorio.* (el laboratorio)

1. Todos los días mis amigos _____. (la cafetería)

2. Los fines de semana mis amigos y yo _____. (el estadio)

3. Después de las clases, mi amigo _____. (el centro estudiantil)

4. Si tengo sueño, yo _____. (la residencia)

5. Cuando no hay clases, yo _____. (el gimnasio)

6. Cuando necesitamos investigar en Internet, mis amigos y yo _____. (la biblioteca)

3.23 **¡Vamos!** Read the statements telling what the following people want to do. Then using the words below tell where they are going. You may use each word only once.

    la biblioteca   **la cafetería**   **la clase**   **el laboratorio**   **la librería**   **el gimnasio**   **la piscina**

1. Yo tengo ganas de nadar. _____

2. Mis amigos tienen ganas de practicar el básquetbol. _____

3. El profesor tiene que enseñar una clase. _____

4. Mis compañeros tienen que buscar información para un proyecto. _____

5. Mi amigo y yo tenemos ganas de comer. _____

6. Una compañera tiene que hacer *(to do)* un experimento. _____

7. Los estudiantes tienen que comprar libros. _____

ir + a + infinitive

3.24 Nuevas estudiantes Mercedes and Daniela are new to the university and they want to experience many of their facilities. Choose from the second column what they are going to do in each place, and then write a complete sentence using the future tense that you have learned (**ir** + **a** + infinitive).

Modelo el estadio, mirar el fútbol
Van a mirar el fútbol.

1. la biblioteca _____

2. la librería _____

3. la cafetería _____

4. el auditorio _____

5. la residencia _____

6. el gimnasio _____

a. asistir a una conferencia

b. tomar una siesta

c. nadar

d. leer

e. hablar con sus amigos y beber café

f. comprar sus libros

3.25 ¿Qué tienen? Read the statements about how the following people feel. Then choose the logical verb to complete the sentence using the future (**ir** + **a** + infinitive). You may use each verb only once.

beber buscar comer correr estudiar recibir tomar

Modelo Mis amigos tienen ganas de ir a una discoteca. *Van a bailar.*

1. Gerardo y Saúl tienen hambre. _____ un sándwich.

2. Lucila tiene sueño. _____ una siesta.

3. Yo tengo prisa. _____ a clase.

4. Mi amiga y yo tenemos éxito en la clase de matemáticas. _____ una buena nota.

5. Mi madre tiene frío. _____ un suéter.

6. Los atletas tienen sed. _____ agua.

7. Mis compañeros tienen miedo de recibir una mala nota. _____ mucho.

3.26 La rutina The following family members have a routine and always do the same thing every day. Read the statements telling what they do routinely, and then tell that they will also do the activity tomorrow.

Modelo Nosotros limpiamos la casa. Mañana también *vamos a limpiar la casa.*

1. Mi esposo corre por la mañana. Mañana también _____.

2. Mis hijos y yo caminamos a la escuela. Mañana también _____.

3. Yo cocino. Mañana también _____.

4. La familia come a las seis. Mañana también _____.

5. Yo miro la tele por la noche. Mañana también _____.

6. Mis hijos leen por la noche. Mañana también _____.

3.27 **¿Qué vas a hacer?** Answer the questions in complete sentences, using **ir** + **a** + infinitive.

¿Qué vas a hacer *(to do)*…

1. hoy por la noche? _____

2. este fin de semana? _____

3. al final del semestre? _____

4. después de terminar *(after finishing)* la universidad? _____

¡Hora de escuchar! 2

3.28 **La hora** Listen to the times mentioned and write the number of the sentence beside the clock that shows the correct time. **¡OJO!** You will not use one of the clocks.

1-27

a. ____

b. ____

c. ____

d. ____

e. ____

f. ____

© Cengage Learning®

3.29 Las actividades You will hear several students talking about their activities. Listen carefully and decide which of the statements makes sense.

1. **a.** Mayte va a estudiar. **b.** Mayte va a comer.

2. **a.** Blanca y Lilian van a viajar. **b.** Blanca y Lilian van a caminar.

3. **a.** Emilio va a aprender a esquiar. **b.** Emilio va a buscar un trabajo.

4. **a.** Germán y Samuel van a regresar a casa. **b.** Germán y Samuel van a correr a clase.

5. **a.** Regina va a comprar ropa. **b.** Regina va a tomar una siesta.

3.30 ¿Cierto o falso? Listen as Reina explains her activities for the week. Then decide if the following statements are true (**cierto**) or false (**falso**).

1. Cierto Falso Reina estudia inglés por la mañana.

2. Cierto Falso Ella trabaja el lunes.

3. Cierto Falso Reina come con su amiga el martes.

4. Cierto Falso Ella corre el miércoles.

5. Cierto Falso Hay una fiesta el sábado.

Pronunciación 2: La *r* y la *rr*

La *r*

When the **r** is not the first letter in a word, it is pronounced similarly to the *tt* in the word *butter* or the *dd* in *ladder*. Listen to the pronunciation of the following words.

derecha   trece   cerca   volver   Veracruz

La *rr*

The letter combination **rr** is rolled. A single **r** at the beginning of a word is pronounced the same as an **rr**. Listen to the pronunciation of the following words.

correo   carro   perro   repetir   Rosa   regalo

The **rr** can be difficult to pronounce. In order to practice trilling, repeat the word *ladder* over and over, faster each time. This is technique will help you learn to make the sound of **rr.**

Un trabalenguas Listen to and repeat the following tongue twister.

Erre con erre cigarro,

Erre con erre barril.

Rápido corren los carros,

Los carros del ferrocarril.

¡Hora de reciclar! 2

3.31 **Los verbos y los posesivos** Complete the paragraph with one of the words in parentheses. Remember, you will need to conjugate the verb to agree with the subject.

Mi familia es muy grande. Nosotros siempre (1.) _____ (celebrar/desear) la Navidad en casa

de (2.) _____ (mi/mis) abuelos. Mi abuela (3.) _____ (preguntar/cocinar) platillos

(dishes) deliciosos. (4.) _____ (Mis/Sus) hermanos y yo (5.) _____ (llegar/comprar)

muchos regalos. (6.) _____ (Nuestro/Nuestra) prima Gloria (7.) _____ (ser/tener)

un año; por eso ella no (8.) _____ (hablar/cantar) muy bien todavía *(yet),* pero ella

(9.) _____ (escuchar/enseñar) música navideña y (10.) _____ (limpiar/bailar).

CAPÍTULO 4 ¿Dónde vives?

Prueba tu vocabulario 1

4.1 **Sopa de letras** Unscramble the letters to form vocabulary words. All of them are places in a city.

1. mcaairfa _____

2. lpetom _____

3. salceeu _____

4. dieoific _____

5. eprrmacouesd _____

6. oclozgóio _____

7. epoarorute _____

8. cifinoa _____

4.2 **Los planes secretos de Mariana** First, use the clues to complete the puzzle. Then combine the letters in the darkened squares to find out where Mariana is planning to go this evening.

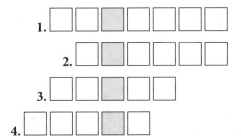

1. Mariana estudia aquí.

2. Mariana compra ropa aquí.

3. Mariana deposita un cheque aquí.

4. A Mariana le gusta ver arte aquí.

4.3 **¿Qué hay en el barrio?** Read each statement below and write the place it describes.

1. En este *(this)* lugar los actores representan obras *(plays)* de Shakespeare. _____

2. En este lugar corres con un amigo, juegas al fútbol o haces *(you have)* un picnic. _____

3. En este lugar compramos comida y otros artículos. _____

4. Las personas pagan por dormir en este lugar. _____

5. A este lugar van las personas que tienen un accidente. _____

6. En este lugar trabajan muchas personas de lunes a viernes. _____

7. A este lugar vamos a rezar. Muchas personas van los domingos. _____

8. A este lugar vamos a nadar en verano. _____

Prueba tu gramática 1 y 2

Stem-changing verbs (o→ue)

4.4 **En la escuela** Everyone is busy at school. Complete the sentences with one of the verbs from the list in order to tell what each student is doing.

almuerza	duerme	encuentra	juega	puede	sueña	vuelve

1. Julio _____ en la cafetería.

2. María Luisa _____ al básquetbol en el gimnasio.

3. Ramón _____ en la clase de sociología porque es aburrida.

4. Santiago no _____ su libro de español en su mochila.

5. Esmeralda _____ al salón de clase.

6. Ivonne no _____ hablar durante el examen de geografía.

4.5 **Mis actividades** Complete the paragraph with the correct form of the verb in parentheses.

Todos los días, después de clase, mi hermana y yo (1.) _____ (almorzar) en casa.

Después yo me (2.) _____ (encontrar) con mis amigas en la biblioteca para estudiar.

Si tenemos tiempo, nosotras (3.) _____ (poder) tomar un café después de estudiar.

El café no (4.) _____ (costar) mucho en el café que está al lado de la biblioteca. Yo

(5.) _____ (volver) a casa a las 8:00 de la noche. Me gusta caminar, pero si *(if)*

(6.) _____ (llover) voy en autobús porque nunca (7.) _____

(recordar) llevar un paraguas conmigo. Cuando llego a casa voy directamente a la cama *(bed),* donde mi

gato y yo (8.) _____ (dormir) calientitos *(warm).*

4.6 **El verbo lógico** Pick the verb that completes each idea logically and write the correct form. **¡OJO!** Pay attention to stem changes.

Magdalena (1.) _____ (soñar / dormir) con viajar mucho. Ahora ella no

(2.) _____ (encontrar / poder) viajar porque estudia y trabaja. Además *(Moreover)*, los

boletos de avión *(airline tickets)* (3.) _____ (almorzar / costar) mucho dinero y ella no

gana *(earns)* mucho dinero. Ella trabaja en un zoológico. Su animal favorito es un chimpancé, porque ella

(4.) _____ (jugar / poder) con él. A Magdalena le gusta su trabajo, excepto cuando

(5.) _____ (morir / llover). Desafortunadamente ella trabaja afuera *(outside)* y

(6.) _____ (volver / llover) mucho en la ciudad donde ella vive.

4.7 **Mis amigos y yo** Choose the most logical conclusion for each sentence. Then write the complete sentence below using the correct form of the verb in parentheses.

1. _____ Cuando yo viajo (dormir)   **a.** los libros a la biblioteca

2. _____ Mis amigos (jugar)   **b.** en un restaurante

3. _____ Mis amigos y yo (almorzar)   **c.** con viajar a la playa

4. _____ Mi amigo (poder)   **d.** nadar en la piscina

5. _____ Yo (soñar)   **e.** en un hotel

6. _____ Tú (devolver)   **f.** al fútbol en el parque

1. _____

2. _____

3. _____

4. _____

5. _____

6. _____

The verb *estar* with prepositions of place

4.8 **El verbo estar** Complete the chart with the appropriate forms of the verb **estar**.

yo _____   nosotros(as) _____

tú _____   vosotros(as) _____

él _____   ellos _____

ella _____   ellas _____

usted _____   ustedes _____

4.9 **Estamos ocupados** Complete the paragraph with the necessary form of the verb **estar.**

Yo (1.) _____ en la universidad hoy. Mi amiga y yo (2.) _____ en

la biblioteca porque necesitamos buscar unos libros. Mi esposo trabaja como farmacéutico, y él

(3.) _____ en la farmacia. Nuestros hijos, Ernesto y Verónica,

(4.) _____ en la escuela. Ernesto (5.) _____ en la escuela primaria

y Verónica (6.) _____ en la escuela secundaria. Y tú, ¿dónde

(7.) _____?

4.10 **¡A dibujar!** Read the statements and create a drawing based on the descriptions. Be sure to read through all the statements before you begin to draw.

1. El hotel está a la izquierda del restaurante.

2. El coche está enfrente del restaurante.

3. La tienda está a la derecha del restaurante.

4. La tienda está entre el restaurante y la biblioteca.

5. El parque está lejos de la biblioteca.

6. Un niño está en el parque.

Nombre _____   Fecha _____

4.11 **¿Dónde están?** Look at the map and tell where the two places are in relation to each other using the verb **estar** and the appropriate preposition.

Modelo el cine / el café
El cine está enfrente del café.

el parque			
la tienda	**el cine**	**el banco**	**el museo**

| **la librería** | **el café** | **la farmacia** | **el teatro** |

© Cengage Learning®

1. el teatro / la tienda _____

2. el cine / el banco _____

3. la farmacia / el café y el teatro _____

4. el parque / la tienda _____

5. el café / la librería _____

6. el museo / el teatro _____

¡Hora de escuchar! 1

2-2

4.12 **En Madrid** Antonio and Miguel are visiting Madrid for the first time. Listen to their conversation and circle all the places that they will visit.

la sinagoga	el parque	el bar	el museo
el teatro	el hotel	el gimnasio	la plaza
el restaurante	el supermercado	la farmacia	el mercado

4.13 **Una foto de mi calle** Toni is showing a picture of the street where his family lives in El Salvador.
2-3 Listen to his description and write down the name of each building on his street. **¡OJO!** One of the buildings will not be labeled.

el banco   la cafetería   la casa de la tía Susana   el correo   la librería   el parque

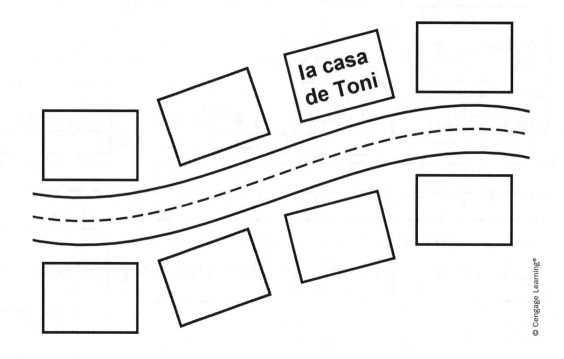

la casa de Toni

© Cengage Learning®

 4.14 **Información turística** You are going to hear a conversation between Graciela, who is a tourist,
2-4 and a man working at the tourist information desk. Listen carefully and decide if the statements below are true (**Cierto**) or false (**Falso**).

1. Cierto Falso   Graciela tiene dos días para visitar la ciudad.

2. Cierto Falso   El Museo de Antropología está detrás de una iglesia.

3. Cierto Falso   Al lado de la iglesia hay una tienda.

4. Cierto Falso   Graciela es de Colombia.

5. Cierto Falso   Graciela necesita un taxi.

Pronunciación 1: La *b* y la *v*

🔊 The **b** and the **v** have very similar sounds in the Spanish language. Many native speakers often have difficulty
2-5 determining which consonant to use when writing. When in the middle of a word, the **v** and the **b** are
pronounced like an English *b* but softer, with the lips barely touching. Listen to the pronunciation of the
following words.

   lluvia   volver   Eva   Fabián   debajo   hablar

La *v*

When at the beginning of a word, the **v** has a *bv* sound. Listen to the pronunciation of the following words.

   viento   vestido   vender   veinte   vamos

Note: Throughout the Spanish-speaking world, there are variations in the pronunciation of the letter **v**.

🔊 **Un trabalenguas** Repeat the following tongue twister.
2-6

De ese bobo vino, nunca beber debe;

vida boba y breve, vivirá si bebe.

¡Hora de reciclar! 1

4.15 **El fin de semana** Complete this conversation by choosing the correct word in parentheses. **¡OJO!**
Be sure to conjugate any verbs.

SAMUEL: ¿Tienes planes para el (1.) _____ (cumpleaños / fin de semana)?

HÉCTOR: Pues, los sábados normalmente mi hermano y yo (2.) _____ (correr / deber) por la

mañana, y por la tarde ayudo a mi papá en su tienda.

SAMUEL: ¿Ah, sí? ¿Y qué (3.) (vender / vivir) ustedes?

HÉCTOR: Es una papelería. (4.) _____ (Abrir / Vender) cuadernos, lápices, bolígrafos…

SAMUEL: ¿Trabajas también los (5.) _____ (martes / domingos)?

HÉCTOR: ¡No, hombre! Los domingos son para pasar con los amigos.

SAMUEL: ¿A ti te (6.) _____ (gustar / creer) los conciertos de rock?

HÉCTOR: Sí, claro. Me (7.) _____ (gustar / aprender) escuchar todo tipo de música.

SAMUEL: Entonces, ¿por qué no (8.) _____ (comprender / asistir) tú y yo al concierto que hay

en la plaza?

HÉCTOR: Muy bien.

¡Hora de escribir!

Write about where you go and what you do on a typical weekend.

Paso 1 Jot down some ideas to incorporate into your paragraph. Think about the following: Where do you live? What is near your house? Where will you go during the weekend (to a store, the bank, a religious service, the supermarket, etc.?) and when? What will you do there?

© Kenneth Sponsler/Shutterstock

Paso 2 Write a paragraph to tell where you will go and what you will do there.

Paso 3 Edit your paragraph:

1. Is your paragraph logically organized or do you skip from one idea to the next?
2. Are you using the correct prepositions of location?
3. Are there any spelling errors?
4. Do verbs agree with the subject?

_____

_____

_____

_____

_____

_____

_____

_____

_____

_____

_____

_____

_____

_____

_____

Prueba tu vocabulario 2

4.16 **Un crucigrama** Complete the following crossword puzzle with the names of the places in the house from the vocabulary list.

© Cengage Learning®

Vertical

1. Es el lugar donde estacionamos el coche.

2. Aquí usamos el inodoro.

3. Es el lugar donde hacemos una barbacoa.

4. Aquí preparamos la comida.

Horizontal

4. Aquí comemos a la mesa.

5. Es la habitación donde hablamos con nuestros visitantes *(visitors)*.

4.17 **Una casa con muchos muebles** Write the name of the items in the room or rooms where you would have them.

la sala	el comedor	
la cocina	el dormitorio	el baño

la cama
el refrigerador
las sillas y la mesa
el sillón
el espejo
el inodoro

la estufa
la alfombra
el microondas
el sofá
la bañera
el armario

la ducha
la mesita de noche
el fregadero
el horno
el lavaplatos
el lavabo

© Cengage Learning®

4.18 **Explicaciones** Read the descriptions and then write the name of the object that is being described. Be sure to include the definite article.

1. Está en el dormitorio y aquí tenemos la ropa. _____

2. Cuando es de noche, necesitamos una para leer y para ver *(to see)*. _____

3. Está en la cocina y lo usamos para cocinar rápidamente. _____

4. Es muy grande y hace frío adentro. _____

5. Está en la sala y es muy cómodo. _____

Prueba tu gramática 3 y 4

Question formation

Interrogatives

4.19 **Interrogativos** Decide which would be the more likely answer for each question word.

1. _____ ¿Dónde?   **a.** La casa a la derecha.

2. _____ ¿Cuándo?   **b.** En la sala.

3. _____ ¿Quién?   **c.** Dos.

4. _____ ¿Cuántos?   **d.** Un espejo.

5. _____ ¿Qué?   **e.** Mañana.

6. _____ ¿Cuál?   **f.** Mi amigo.

4.20 **Un apartamento nuevo** Avelina is going to rent a new apartment, and her friend Rosalba has a lot of questions. Complete her questions with the most logical interrogative words.

Rosalba: ¿ (1.) _____ dormitorios tiene tu apartamento?

Avelina: Tiene tres dormitorios.

Rosalba: ¿ (2.) _____ te vas a mudar *(to move)*?

Avelina: Me voy a mudar la próxima semana.

Rosalba: ¿Con (3.) _____ vas a vivir?

Avelina: Voy a vivir con mi amiga Samantha.

Rosalba: ¿ (4.) _____ van a pagar por el alquiler *(rent)*?

Avelina: Vamos a pagar cinco mil pesos.

Rosalba: ¿ (5.) _____ está tu nuevo apartamento?

Avelina: Está en el barrio Colón.

4.21 Preguntas Amalia has just moved to a new city and has just moved in with her friend Sandra. Complete their conversation by supplying the questions.

AMALIA: ¿ (1.) _____?

SANDRA: Tengo <u>tres clases</u> este semestre.

AMALIA: ¿ (2.) _____?

SANDRA: <u>Historia</u> es mi clase favorita.

AMALIA: ¿ (3.) _____?

SANDRA: Voy a trabajar <u>en un supermercado</u>. Oye, cambiando de tema *(changing subject),* el apartamento es

muy grande. ¿ (4.) _____?

AMALIA: Hay <u>tres</u> dormitorios.

SANDRA: ¿ (5.) _____?

AMALIA: Tu dormitorio <u>está a la izquierda de la sala</u>.

SANDRA: ¿ (6.) _____?

AMALIA: Debemos pagar el alquiler <u>el primer día de cada *(each)* mes</u>.

4.22 La casa nueva Imagine you just moved to a house that you will be sharing with a friend. Ask him/her logical questions using the question words in parentheses.

1. (dónde) _____

2. (cuándo) _____

3. (quién) _____

4. (cómo) _____

5. (cuál) _____

6. (qué) _____

Stem changing verbs (e→ie) and (e→i)

4.23 **Completar** Choose the word that best completes each sentence.

Los estudiantes…

1. (piden / preguntan) si hay un examen.

2. (piensan de / piensan en) las vacaciones de verano.

3. (piden / preguntan) crédito extra.

4. (comienzan / comienzan a) leer la novela.

5. (piensan / piensan de) escribir mensajes después de *(after)* clase.

6. (empiezan / empiezan a) las composiciones.

7. (piden / preguntan) ayuda con la tarea.

8. (piensan en / piensan) estudiar en la biblioteca.

9. (piden / preguntan) cuál es la fecha.

10. (empiezan / empiezan a) escribir la tarea.

4.24 **En el nuevo apartamento** Bárbara and her friend are moving into a new apartment. Complete the sentences about their activities using the verbs from the list below. You may use each verb only once.

cerrar	comenzar	empezar	encender	pensar
perder	preferir	querer	reír	servir

Bárbara y su amiga llegan a su apartamento y (1.) _____ a poner *(to put)* todos

los muebles en sus habitaciones. Es un día de invierno y hace mucho frío, por eso Bárbara

(2.) _____ las ventanas y ella (3.) _____ la calefacción *(heater)*.

Cuando terminan, ellas tienen mucha hambre. Bárbara (4.) _____ pedir una pizza, pero

su amiga (5.) _____ comer algo más saludable *(healthy)* y ella prepara una sopa. Bárbara

(6.) _____ la sopa y las dos amigas comen y (7) _____ mucho.

¡Les gusta mucho su nuevo apartamento!

4.25 **Mis actividades** Complete the paragraph with the correct form of the verb in parentheses.

¡Me encanta el invierno! Cuando (1.) _____ (empezar) a nevar, me gusta esquiar en las

montañas, aunque a veces *(sometimes)* yo (2.) _____ (preferir) leer un buen libro en

casa. También me gusta el verano porque las vacaciones (3.) _____ (comenzar) en junio.

En julio yo (4.) _____ (pensar) ir de excursión a la playa con mis amigos. Nosotros

(5.) _____ (querer) acampar *(to camp)* por tres días. Siempre que estamos en la playa,

nosotros (6.) _____ (encender) la radio y bailamos. Cuando estoy con mis amigos, yo

siempre (7.) _____ (reír) mucho porque son muy cómicos.

_____

4.26 **Daniela y yo** Form complete sentences by combining the elements.

> **Modelo** nosotras / perder / la tarea
> *Nosotras perdemos la tarea.*

1. Daniela y yo / pensar / estudiar para la clase de matemáticas _____

2. Daniela / preferir / estudiar en la sala _____

3. yo / querer / ir a mi dormitorio _____

4. ella / entender / las matemáticas muy bien _____

5. más tarde/ nosotras / encender / la tele _____

¡Hora de escuchar! 2

4.27 **En la casa** You will hear a description of a new house. Listen carefully and decide if the statements
2-7   below are true (**Cierto**) or false (**Falso**).

1. Cierto   Falso   La familia pasa mucho tiempo en el jardín de la casa.

2. Cierto   Falso   Hay un baño en la planta baja.

3. Cierto   Falso   No hay microondas en la cocina.

4. Cierto   Falso   No hay televisor en el dormitorio.

◀)) **4.28** **Respuestas lógicas** Listen to the questions and choose the most logical response.
2-8

1. **a.** En un apartamento.

   b. De Guatemala.

   c. Dos personas.

2. **a.** No cuesta mucho.

   b. Es pequeño pero bonito.

   c. Es el apartamento de mis padres.

3. **a.** Cerca de la universidad.

   b. En la sala.

   c. Con un amigo.

4. **a.** Todos los días.

   b. Dos.

   c. Dormir.

5. **a.** Un microondas y una cafetera.

   b. Al lado del comedor.

   c. Por la mañana.

◀)) **4.29** **Busco habitación** Mercedes is looking for a room to rent in a house in Quito, Ecuador. She called
2-9 and left a message with questions about the house. The owner of the house responded and left a message
with the answers. Listen to the owner's message and use the information to answer the questions that
Mercedes had asked.

1. ¿Cuántos dormitorios hay? _____

2. ¿Qué muebles hay en la habitación que alquilan? _____

3. ¿Hay un baño privado para la habitación que alquilan? _____

4. ¿Qué electrodomésticos puede usar? _____

5. ¿Cuántas personas viven en la casa? _____

6. ¿Cuánto cuesta el alquiler? _____

Pronunciación 2: la *c* y la *g*

La *c*

🔊
2-10
A **c** before an **a, o,** or **u** has a *k* sound as in *keep*. This is known as a hard **c.** In Latin America, a **c** before an **e** or an **i** has an *s* sound as in *soup*. This is known as a soft **c.** However, in Spain a **c** before an **e** or an **i** is pronounced with a *th* sound, as in *think*.

Listen to the pronunciation of the following words.

coco	cuarenta	casa	cama	cuesta
celebrar	cierro	trece	gracias	difícil

La *g*

The **g** is also soft in front of an **e** or an **i,** and is pronounced similar to the *h* sound in *help*. When in front of any other vowel (**a, o,** or **u**) or a consonant, the **g** has a hard sound, like the *g* in *dog*.

Listen to the pronunciation of the following words.

generoso	gimnasio	Gilberto	inteligente	general
gorro	Galicia	Magda	seguir	tengo

🔊
2-11
Pronounce the following words, paying attention to the **g** and **c.** Then listen to the CD to check your pronunciation.

cocodrilo	ciencia	cántaro	centenario	Cándida
general	guitarra	gigante	geografía	hamburguesa

¡Hora de reciclar! 2

4.30 **En casa** The Suárez family is at home today. Read the statements to find out where they are in the house. Then choose a logical verb from the list and tell what they are going to do there. You may use each verb only once.

cocinar   **jugar con el perro**   **mirar la tele**   **tomar una siesta**   **trabajar en el auto**

Modelo   Mi madre está en el patio. *Va a leer.*

1. Estoy en la cocina. _____

2. Los niños están en el jardín. _____

3. Mi esposo está en el garaje. _____

4. Mi padre está en el dormitorio. _____

5. Mi hija está en la sala. _____

CAPÍTULO 5   ¿Estás feliz en el trabajo?

Prueba tu vocabulario 1

5.1 **Reacciones lógicas** Match the first column with the most logical ending.

1. _____ José está en el estadio de fútbol. Está…

2. _____ Nayeli y Miriam están en su oficina. Están…

3. _____ Lidia tiene muchos problemas en su trabajo. Está…

4. _____ Nosotros tenemos tres trabajos diferentes. Estamos…

5. _____ Bruno canta y luego llora (cries), ríe y habla solo. Está…

a. frustrada.

b. loco.

c. cansados.

d. divertido.

e. ocupadas.

5.2 **Una telenovela** You are the director of a soap opera and are telling the actors and actresses how their characters are feeling so they can act with emotion. Complete each sentence with a logical adjective.

1. Marco Aurelio, tu mejor amigo piensa besar a tu novia. Estás _____.

2. Laura, tienes un esposo excelente, un buen trabajo y una casa bonita. Estás _____.

3. José, tú sabes (know) que tienes razón. Estás _____.

4. Calia, no encuentras tu anillo (ring) favorito y cuesta más de $1000. Estás _____.

5. Sra. Ramírez, usted padece (suffer) de insomnio. Está _____.

5.3 **Estados de ánimo** Using the verb **estar** and one of the adjectives in the list, describe how the following people are feeling. ¡OJO! Pay attention to adjective agreement.

cansado   celoso   enfermo   nervioso   sorprendido

Modelo   Los Gómez tienen una casa nueva.
Están contentos.

1. Es el cumpleaños de Víctor y sus amigos le preparan una fiesta sorpresa.

   (Víctor) _____

2. José tiene una entrevista para conseguir un nuevo trabajo.

   _____

3. Lola ve a su esposo hablando con una chica muy guapa.

   _____

4. Jaime y Héctor acaban de correr un maratón.

   _____

5. Joaquín está en el hospital.

   _____

5.4 **Asociaciones** Write a sentence expressing how you might feel in each of the places in the list below and explain why.

Modelo   el hospital   *Estoy triste porque hay personas enfermas.*

1. el cine _____

2. el bar _____

3. la iglesia _____

4. la universidad _____

5. la playa _____

6. el museo _____

Prueba tu gramática 1 y 2

Estar with adjectives and with present progressive

5.5 **Un mensaje** You are instant messaging with your best friend, who wants to know exactly what is going on around you. Complete the text message and write the verbs in present progressive form. The first one has been done for you.

Hola, Isabel. Ahora mismo yo ___*estoy mirando*___ (mirar) la televisión. Mi mamá está en la cocina; ella

(1.) _____ (preparar) la comida. Mi papá (2.) _____ (leer) el periódico y mis

hermanos (3.) _____ (jugar) dominó. Ellos también (4.) _____ (pelear – *to fight*).

Nuestro gato (5.) _____ (comer), y yo (6.) _____ (beber) un refresco.

5.6 **La actividad más lógica** Read the description of the following situations, and then write down the activity that you think the people are doing. Choose the most logical activity from the list below.

nadar en el mar   **mirar una película**   **bailar en una fiesta**

comer un sándwich   **dormir**   **estudiar**

> **Modelo**   Laura tiene frío. → (beber un chocolate caliente)
> *Laura está bebiendo un chocolate caliente.*

1. Miguel y Dolores van a tener un examen muy difícil mañana. _____

2. Micaela celebra su cumpleaños hoy. _____

3. Yo estoy en Cancún. _____

4. Tú estás en el cine. _____

5. El profesor está en un café. _____

6. Nosotros estamos en nuestra casa. _____

5.7 **En la sala de espera** The people in the picture are in the waiting room at a doctor's office. Using the present progressive, tell what each person is doing.

1. _____

2. _____

3. _____

4. _____

5. _____

5.8 **¿Qué estás haciendo?** Your friend calls you a few times on your cell phone and asks what you are doing. Each time he calls, you are doing something different. Using the verbs in parentheses in the present progressive, tell him what you are doing.

1. Estoy en la cocina. (limpiar la estufa) _____

2. Estoy en la sala. (leer el periódico) _____

3. Estoy en el jardín. (beber una limonada) _____

4. Estoy en un café. (hablar con amigos) _____

5. Estoy en mi dormitorio. (jugar videojuegos) _____

Ser and *estar*

5.9 **Mi amiga Susana** Decide which verb best completes the sentences below.

Susana…

1. (es / está) mi mejor amiga.

2. (es / está) secretaria.

3. (es / está) en la oficina ahora.

4. (es / está) muy ocupada.

5. (es / está) feliz en su trabajo.

6. (es / está) de Caracas, Venezuela.

7. (es / está) una chica muy lista.

8. (es / está) muy guapa hoy.

5.10 **¿Ser o estar?… esa es la pregunta** Betty is writing an e-mail to a new friend in El Salvador. Complete her e-mail with the correct form of the verb **ser** or **estar**.

Querido Armando:

Gracias por escribir. Yo también (1.) _____ estudiante en la universidad, y

(2.) _____ muy ocupada. (3.) _____ muy alta y tengo el pelo negro. Vivo

con mis padres, pero aquí en los Estados Unidos no (4.) _____ muy común vivir con los

padres. Mi padre (5.) _____ policía y mi madre (6.) _____ arquitecta,

pero ahora ella (7.) _____ enferma y por eso hoy ella (8.) _____ en casa.

Hoy (9.) _____ lunes y yo tengo mucho trabajo, pero quiero escribirte otra vez muy pronto.

¡Yo (10.) _____ feliz de ser tu amiga!

5.11 **Oraciones incompletas** Choose the best word or phrase to complete each sentence. **¡OJO!** Pay attention to the verb.

1. **a.** Yo soy (estudiante / estudiando).

   b. Yo estoy (inteligente / ocupado).

2. **a.** Mi mejor amiga es (enamorada / simpática).

   b. Mi mejor amiga está (de Panamá / en Panamá).

3. **a.** Mi profesor es (enfrente de la clase / trabajador).

   b. Mi profesor está (hablando por teléfono / español).

4. **a.** El presidente es (político / en la Casa Blanca).

   b. El presidente está (preocupado / liberal).

5.12 **En el trabajo** Look at the picture and write six sentences to describe it. You should use **ser** in three of the sentences and **estar** in the other three.

1. _____

_____

2. _____

_____

3. _____

_____

4. _____

_____

5. _____

_____

6. _____

_____

¡Hora de escuchar! 1

◀)) **5.13** **¿Cómo están?** You will hear six different people talking about a situation they are in. Decide
2-12 which of the following statements best describes how each person feels and write the appropriate
name(s) from the list below in the space provided.

Dora   Gloria   Miranda y Eliseo   Pedro   Roberto y José   Salma

1. _____ está preocupado y nervioso.

2. _____ está contenta.

3. _____ están cansados.

4. _____ están felices.

5. _____ está avergonzada.

6. _____ está preocupada.

_____

◀)) **5.14** **Preguntas** Choose the best answer to each of the questions you hear. ¡OJO! Pay attention to the verb.
2-13

1. **a.** Soy alto.   **b.** Estoy bien, gracias.   **c.** Estoy estudiando.

2. **a.** Soy de Bolivia.   **b.** Estoy en mi casa.   **c.** Está nublado.

3. **a.** Es de Florida.   **b.** Está bien.   **c.** Es Gerardo.

4. **a.** Está triste.   **b.** Es muy simpático.   **c.** Está trabajando.

5. **a.** Está cansado.   **b.** Es de Colombia.   **c.** Está en la universidad.

_____

◀)) **5.15** **Confesiones** Listen as Estela tells you a little about herself, and then decide if the statements below
2-14 are true (**cierto**) or false (**falso**).

1. Cierto   Falso   Estela vive con su mejor amiga.

2. Cierto   Falso   Estela es de Colombia.

3. Cierto   Falso   Estela está enamorada y quiere casarse (*to get married*).

4. Cierto   Falso   Su novio también es de Colombia.

5. Cierto   Falso   Estela está estudiando.

Pronunciación 1: la *d*

🔊 In Spanish, the letter **d** has two different pronunciations. At the beginning of a phrase or a sentence or after an **n** or
2-15 an **l,** it is pronounced similarly to the English *d* in *dish.* Listen to the pronunciation of the following words.

¿De quién?   ¿Dígame?   igualdad   el día   ¿Dónde está?   comiendo

In all other cases, the **d** is pronounced like the English *th* in *other.* Listen to the pronunciation of the following
words.

Buenos días.   Ecuador   adiós   video   nada   a las doce

🔊 **Un trabalenguas** Listen to and repeat the following tongue twister.
2-16 Dicen que dan doce docenas de dulces

donde dar debieran diez discos dorados.

Si donde debieran dar discos dorados,

dan dulces o donas.

¡Hora de reciclar! 1

5.16 **Las preposiciones** Look at the drawing. For each pair of items, write a sentence telling where the
first item is in relation to the other. Be sure to use at least four different prepositions.

© Cengage Learning®

1. la mesita de noche / la cama _____

2. la lámpara / la mesita de noche _____

3. la silla / la cama _____

4. los libros / la cama _____

5. la lámpara / el espejo _____

6. la alfombra / la mesita de noche _____

¡Hora de escribir!

Tomorrow you are starting a job in this restaurant. Write a journal entry about your new job.

Paso 1 Jot down some ideas to incorporate into your journal entry. Think about the following: What type of restaurant is it? What will you do? What days and hours will you work? How are you feeling about starting work tomorrow? What are you doing right now to prepare for your first day?

© Diego Cervo/Shutterstock

Paso 2 Write a paragraph using the information you generated in **Paso 1**.

Paso 3 Edit your paragraph:

   1. Is your paragraph logically organized or do you skip from one idea to the next?
   2. Are there any short sentences you can combine by using **y** or **pero**?
   3. Are there any spelling errors?
   4. Do verbs agree with the subject?
   5. Do adjectives agree with the nouns they describe?

_____

_____

_____

_____

_____

_____

_____

_____

_____

_____

_____

_____

_____

_____

_____

_____

_____

Prueba tu vocabulario 2

5.17 **Sopa de letras** Unscramble the letters. All the words are professions.

1. zatirc _____

5. nogeeniir _____

2. odobaga _____

6. sidroñade _____

3. moferrene _____

7. oraesctrie _____

4. torofógaf _____

8. ntntaace _____

5.18 **La agencia de empleos** You work in an employment agency and are helping to find the right jobs for your clients. Read the descriptions and write the name of the profession you think they should have.

agente de viajes   arquitecto   asistente de vuelo

cocinero   maestro   pintor   policía   político

1. _____ Cocina muy bien.

2. _____ Conoce (Knows) bien toda la ciudad y mantiene (keeps) el orden.

3. _____ Quiere trabajar con niños y tiene mucha paciencia.

4. _____ Habla varias lenguas y le gusta viajar.

5. _____ Le gusta diseñar casas y edificios.

6. _____ Sabe (Knows how) usar la computadora y es experto en turismo.

7. _____ Le gusta hablar en público y es experto en cuestiones sociales.

8. _____ Es artista y le gusta expresarse con imágenes.

5.19 **En el trabajo** Complete each statement with a logical profession from the vocabulary list in this chapter. **¡OJO!** Pay attention to the gender of the profession.

1. El _____ está enseñando a los niños.

2. El _____ está jugando fútbol en el estadio.

3. El _____ está hablando frente a muchas personas porque quiere sus votos.

4. El _____ está escribiendo un artículo para el periódico.

5. La _____ está sirviendo comida en el restaurante.

6. La _____ está examinando a un paciente en el hospital.

7. La _____ está reparando un coche en su taller (garage).

8. El _____ está abordando el avión.

Prueba tu gramática 3 y 4

Verbs with changes in the first person

5.20 **Adivina quién lo dice** Guess the profession of the people that are talking. In order to know what they are saying, you will need to conjugate the verb in parentheses in the first person (**yo**).

1. la _____: Yo les _____ (traer) la comida y bebidas a los pasajeros del avión.

2. el _____: Yo _____ (poner) la ropa de la tienda en orden.

3. el _____: Yo les _____ (dar) consejos (*advice*) a las personas que tienen problemas.

4. la _____: Yo _____ (decir) las noticias (*news*) en la televisión.

5. el _____: Yo _____ (conducir) un automóvil blanco y negro muy rápido.

6. la _____: Yo _____ (hacer) una comida deliciosa para mis clientes.

7. el _____: Yo _____ (oír) la música y bailo.

8. la _____: Yo _____ (venir) a la corte para defender a mi cliente.

5.21 **Un poco de lógica** Decide which of the verbs logically completes the following sentences. Then write the verb in the first person. **¡OJO!** You will not use all the verbs.

conducir	decir	hacer	poner	salir	seguir	traer	ver

1. Soy piloto y _____ muchos viajes.

2. Soy periodista y _____ la verdad (*truth*).

3. Soy taxista y _____ un taxi.

4. Soy mesera y _____ las mesas en el restaurante.

5. Soy crítico de cine y _____ muchas películas.

6. Soy médica y _____ del hospital muy tarde.

7. Soy secretario y _____ las instrucciones de mi jefe.

5.22 **Una entrevista con el consejero** In many countries, students finishing high school interview with a counselor to identify the best career for them. Complete the student's answers with the verb used in the question in the first person (**yo**) form.

1. **Pregunta:** ¿Dices la verdad? **Respuesta:** Sí, siempre _____ la verdad.

2. **Pregunta:** ¿Conduces bien? **Respuesta:** Sí, _____ muy bien.

3. **Pregunta:** ¿Pones todo en orden en tu casa? **Respuesta:** Sí, _____ todo en orden una vez al mes.

4. **Pregunta:** ¿Das muchos consejos? **Respuesta:** A veces _____ consejos.

5. **Pregunta:** ¿Haces muchos viajes? **Respuesta:** Sí, _____ muchos viajes.

6. **Pregunta:** ¿Ves muchas películas? **Respuesta:** No, no _____ muchas películas.

5.23 **¿Qué hacen?** Conjugate the verb according to the subject, and then choose a logical ending from the list below.

al cine	un auto viejo	varias películas	la tarea
música	comida a la clase	~~mentiras~~	

Modelo   (decir) Tú *dices mentiras.*

1. (ver) Yo _____.

2. (hacer) Los estudiantes _____.

3. (conducir) Mi amigo _____.

4. (traer) El profesor de español _____.

5. (salir) Yo _____.

6. (oír) Tú _____.

Saber *and* conocer

5.24 **Algunas preguntas** The university is planning to hire a new Spanish instructor, and the committee is writing the questions for the interview. Decide which verb best completes each sentence.

1. ¿ (Sabe / Conoce) usted la historia de España?

2. ¿ (Sabe / Conoce) usted enseñar una clase?

3. ¿ (Sabe / Conoce) usted a los estudiantes?

4. ¿ (Sabe / Conoce) usted usar una computadora?

5. ¿ (Sabe / Conoce) usted la universidad?

6. ¿ (Sabe / Conoce) usted quién es el jefe del departamento?

5.25 **¿Quién es?** Find the most logical match for each profession and create logical sentences. Remember to conjugate the verbs.

1. los policías   escribir bien

2. la actriz   reparar *(to repair)* vehículos

3. los mecánicos   **saber**   la ciudad

4. el periodista   **conocer**   al director

5. la cocinera   dónde están todos los artículos de la tienda

6. el dependiente   preparar buena comida

1. _____

2. _____

3. _____

4. _____

5. _____

6. _____

5.26 **La entrevista de trabajo** Use the correct forms of the verbs **saber** and **conocer** to complete the interview.

SR. SÁNCHEZ: Buenas tardes, Sra. Amado. ¿(1.) _____ usted a mi secretaria? Ella va a

tomar notas mientras nosotros hablamos.

SRA. AMADO: Mucho gusto.

SR. SÁNCHEZ: Bien, señora, ¿usted (2.) _____ qué hacemos en esta compañía?

SRA. AMADO: Sí, yo (3.) _____ que ustedes exportan ropa a toda Latinoamérica. Mi hija

dice que ustedes (4.) _____ hacer la mejor ropa del mundo.

SR. SÁNCHEZ: Muy bien. En este trabajo es necesario viajar mucho. ¿Usted (5.) _____

bien todo el país?

SRA. AMADO: Yo (6.) _____ bien el Perú, pero no (7.) _____ otros

países.

SR. SÁNCHEZ: Bueno, yo (8.) _____ que usted es la persona perfecta para este trabajo.

¡Bienvenida!

5.27 **Oraciones incompletas** Choose the logical option to complete the following sentences.

1. El mesero conoce _____.   **a.** servir la comida   **b.** el restaurante

2. La deportista sabe _____.   **a.** dónde está el estadio   **b.** muchos deportistas famosos

3. La pintora sabe _____.   **a.** pintar   **b.** muchos artistas famosos

4. El médico conoce _____.   **a.** explicar las enfermedades   **b.** a sus pacientes

5. El secretario sabe _____.   **a.** la oficina   **b.** el nombre de la esposa de su jefe

6. La maestra conoce _____.   **a.** bien a sus estudiantes   **b.** ser muy paciente

¡Hora de escuchar! 2

5.28 **Las profesiones** You will hear information about the following people's work. Listen carefully
2-17   and match the names with the place where they most likely work.

1. _____ José   **a.** la escuela

2. _____ Miriam   **b.** el laboratorio

3. _____ Laura   **c.** la oficina

4. _____ Marcelo   **d.** el aeropuerto

5. _____ Valeria   **e.** el hospital

5.29 **Preguntas** You just met a classmate in the library while you are studying. Answer his questions.
2-18

1. _____

2. _____

3. _____

4. _____

5.30 **No estoy contento** Listen to the conversation between two friends and answer the questions.
2-19

1. ¿Por qué José no está contento hoy?
   a. Está enfermo.   **b.** No tiene trabajo.   **c.** Tiene mucho trabajo.

2. ¿Dónde trabaja Manuel?
   a. en un restaurante   **b.** en una oficina de turismo   **c.** en una biblioteca

3. ¿Qué debe saber José para obtener el trabajo?
   a. usar computadoras   **b.** hablar inglés   **c.** vender mapas a los turistas

4. ¿Con quién debe hablar José mañana?
   a. con el jefe de Manuel   **b.** con un mesero   **c.** con el cocinero

Pronunciación 2: la *x*

🔊 While there are variations throughout different Latin American countries, normally the letter **x** is pronounced
2-20 like the *x* in the English word *exit*. Listen to the pronunciation of the following words:

     exagerar   existir   exótico   exultar   exhalar

When it is at the beginning of a word or before a consonant it is usually pronounced like an *s*, such as in the
English word *simple*. Listen to the pronunciation of the following words:

     xenofobia   xilófono   experimentar   extremo   excepto

The letter **x** in words that originated in Náhuatl (an indigenous language of Mexico) is pronounced like the *h*
in *hot*. Listen to the pronunciation of the following words:

     mexicano   Oaxaca   Xalapa

🔊 Read through the following sentences, paying particular attention to the pronunciation of the **x.** Then listen to
2-21 the audio to verify your pronunciation.

1. El experto tiene el número exacto.

2. Mi experiencia en México fue excelente.

3. A una persona xenofóbica no le gustan los extranjeros.

¡Hora de reciclar! 2

5.31 **La entrevista** Write the logical questions to complete the conversation between the interviewer
and Zoila, the interviewee. **¡OJO!** You will need to use **usted** since this is a formal relationship.

El jefe: Buenos días. (1.) ¿_____?

Zoila: <u>Estoy bien</u> gracias.

El jefe: (2.) ¿_____?

Zoila: Estoy interesada en el trabajo <u>porque es una buena compañía</u>.

El jefe: (3.) ¿_____?

Zoila: Trabajo <u>en una compañía internacional</u>.

El jefe: (4.) ¿_____?

Zoila: Mi jefa es <u>la señora Gómez</u>.

El jefe: (5.) ¿_____?

Zoila: Trabajo <u>con ocho personas</u>.

El jefe: (6.) ¿_____?

Zoila: Puedo empezar a trabajar <u>el lunes</u>.

El jefe: Muy bien. Voy a tomar una decisión muy pronto.

CAPÍTULO **6**   ¿Cómo pasas el día?

Prueba tu vocabulario 1

6.1 **Asociaciones** Match each activity to the part of the body that is associated with it.

1. _____ pensar   **a.** los dientes

2. _____ ver   **b.** las piernas

3. _____ comer   **c.** las orejas

4. _____ escribir   **d.** los ojos

5. _____ oír   **e.** la cabeza

6. _____ caminar   **f.** la mano

6.2 **¿Qué es?** Write the part of the body indicated in the drawing. Include the definite article.

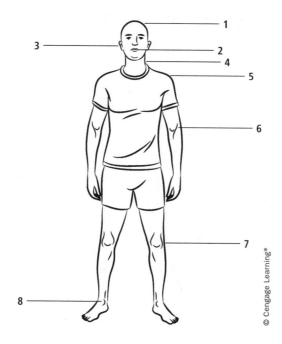

© Cengage Learning®

1. _____   5. _____

2. _____   6. _____

3. _____   7. _____

4. _____   8. _____

6.3 **Las partes del cuerpo** Read each definition and write down the part of the body it describes. Include the definite article.

1. _____ Tenemos veinte en total, cinco en cada (each) mano y en cada pie.

2. _____ Está en la cara, entre los ojos.

3. _____ Está en medio del brazo.

4. _____ Están dentro de la boca y son blancos.

5. _____ Los ojos y la boca están en ella.

6. _____ Está detrás y no podemos ver esta parte del cuerpo.

6.4 **¿Cuál es el verbo?** Choose the most logical verb to complete each sentence.

1. Todos los días Juan tiene que (levantarse / dormirse / acostarse) a las seis de la mañana.

2. Pedro tiene que (maquillarse / ducharse / quitarse la ropa) antes de ir a su trabajo todas las mañanas.

3. Sofía prefiere (peinarse / acostarse / levantarse) en el baño.

4. El profesor quiere (despertarse / sentarse / lavarse) en su silla.

5. Es importante (cepillarse / maquillarse / vestirse) los dientes.

6. Antes de ducharse, es buena idea (vestirse / quitarse la ropa / sentarse).

6.5 **El orden lógico** Put each group of verbs in the most logical order as part of a daily routine.

Modelo   levantarse, estirarse, arreglarse
           estirarse, levantarse, arreglarse

1. secarse, ducharse, vestirse _____

2. ponerse la pijama, dormirse, acostarse _____

3. secarse la cara, maquillarse, lavarse la cara _____

4. peinarse, secarse el pelo, lavarse el pelo _____

5. ducharse, levantarse, despertarse _____

Prueba tu gramática 1 y 2

Reflexive verbs

6.6 **Descripciones** Look at the illustrations and complete the sentences using the present tense of reflexive verbs to describe what the person does every day.

Modelo   Mi padre ____*se afeita*____.

1. Mi hijo _____.

2. Mi tía _____.

3. Mi abuela _____.

4. Mi primo _____.

5. Mis hermanas _____.

6. Mi gato _____.

6.7 **De vacaciones** Cuauhtémoc, Zacarías, and Saúl are on vacation in a small hotel. They are making plans for the morning so that they will not be in each other's way. Complete their ideas with the correct form of the verb in parentheses. **¡OJO!** Some verbs will remain in the infinitive.

Cuauhtémoc: Mañana debemos (1.) _____ (despertarse) muy temprano.

Este es el plan: yo (2.) _____ (ducharse) primero y (3.) _____

(lavarse) el pelo en la ducha. Mientras yo (4.) _____ (cepillarse) los dientes, Zacarías

(5.) _____ (vestirse) y (6.) _____ (peinarse).

Saúl: Es una buena idea. Y mientras ustedes (7.) _____ (ducharse) y

(8.) _____ (vestirse), yo puedo (9.) _____ (sentarse) a leer el periódico.

Zacarías: ¡Perfecto! Así todos (10.) _____ (irse) a la playa antes de las diez de la mañana.

6.8 **Preguntas personales** Answer the questions in complete sentences.

Modelo ¿Cuántas veces (times) a la semana te afeitas?
Me afeito tres veces a la semana.

1. ¿Cuántas veces a la semana te lavas el pelo?

_____

2. ¿Con qué champú te lavas el pelo?

_____

3. ¿Con qué jabón te lavas las manos?

_____

4. ¿Con qué pasta de dientes te cepillas los dientes?

_____

5. ¿Qué colonia o perfume te pones?

_____

6. ¿Cuántas veces a la semana te afeitas (la cara o las piernas)?

_____

6.9 **Las rutinas de los famosos** Decide which of the verbs below logically completes each sentence. Then write the verb in its correct form. **¡OJO!** Not all the verbs will take the reflexive form.

estirar(se)   lavar(se)   levantar(se)   maquillar(se)   poner(se)   sentar(se)

1. Salma Hayek y Penélope Cruz _____ antes de filmar una escena.

2. Carlos Fuentes _____ al escritorio para escribir.

3. Fernando Alonso _____ el coche antes de la carrera *(race)*.

4. Shakira _____ antes de empezar a bailar.

5. Tony González _____ pesas *(weights)* para mantenerse en forma.

6. Vladimir Guerrero _____ el uniforme antes de jugar al béisbol.

6.10 **¿Qué están haciendo?** Look at the pictures and write complete sentences indicating what the people are doing, using the present progressive. **¡OJO!** Not all of the verbs will be in the reflexive form.

1.
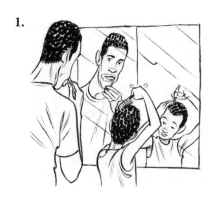

2.

3.
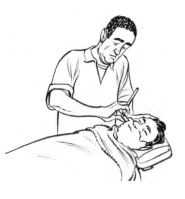

4.

5.

© Cengage Learning®

1. _____

2. _____

3. _____

4. _____

5. _____

Adverbs of time and frequency

6.11 La opción lógica Read about Carmela's routine and complete the sentences with the most logical word.

1. Normalmente Carmela se despierta y _____ se levanta.
   a. antes   **b.** después

2. _____ practica yoga en la mañana.
   a. Todavía   **b.** A veces

3. Carmela está duchándose _____.
   a. más tarde   **b.** ahora

4. _____ se ducha escucha música.
   a. Mientras   **b.** Pronto

5. _____ va a secarse el pelo.
   a. Luego   **b.** Mientras

6. Carmela _____ se maquilla.
   a. ya   **b.** siempre

6.12 La rutina Complete the paragraph about Cristina's routine by writing the expression that completes the ideas logically and correctly. **¡OJO!** Use each expression only once.

antes	antes de	después	después de	mientras	normalmente
todavía	ya	ya no			

Cristina se despierta a las cinco de la mañana y (1.) _____ se ducha y se viste.

(2.) _____ vestirse va a la cocina y prepara su desayuno (breakfast).

(3.) _____ come, Cristina bebe café y lee el periódico. (4.) _____ salir para el trabajo, le sirve comida a su perro. Son las siete de la mañana cuando ella sale de su casa, pero sus dos compañeras (5.) _____ duermen. Ellas se levantan más tarde.

(6.) _____ Cristina regresa a su casa a las dos de la tarde. A esa hora ella

(7.) _____ tiene mucha hambre, así que se prepara una comida grande. A las cuatro Cristina tiene que regresar a su trabajo, pero (8.) _____ toma una siesta corta para no estar muy cansada en la oficina. Vuelve a su casa a las ocho y (9.) _____ sale, excepto si sus amigos la invitan a hacer algo.

6.13 Dos rutinas Gabriel's routine is very different from Jorge's. Complete their dialogue, choosing the adverbs that best complete the sentences.

JORGE: (1.) (Mientras / Mañana) me voy a levantar tarde porque es sábado.

GABRIEL: ¡Qué suerte! Yo (2.) (luego / casi nunca) puedo levantarme tarde los fines de semana porque tengo un nuevo trabajo y (3.) (normalmente / pronto) empiezo a trabajar a las ocho de la mañana.

JORGE: Yo sé que tengo mucha suerte porque puedo levantarme tarde. Además, yo (4.) (todavía / ya no) tomo clases y no tengo que levantarme temprano (5.) (casi nunca / antes de). Ahora trabajo (6.) (hoy / todos los días), pero me gusta mucho mi trabajo y tengo un horario flexible.

6.14 ¿Con qué frecuencia? Tell how often you do the following activities.

Modelo   ducharse   *Me ducho una vez al día. / Me ducho todos los días.*

1. levantarse temprano _____

2. salir a divertirse con amigos _____

3. ponerse ropa elegante _____

4. acostarse después de medianoche _____

5. afeitarse (la cara o las piernas) _____

¡Hora de escuchar! 1

6.15 ¿Es lógico? Listen to the statements and decide if they are logical (**lógico**) or illogical (**ilógico**).
2-22

1. lógico   ilógico

2. lógico   ilógico

3. lógico   ilógico

4. lógico   ilógico

5. lógico   ilógico

6. lógico   ilógico

6.16 Respuestas You will hear five questions. Write the letter of the most logical answer for each one.
2-23

1. _____   **a.** Luego.   **b.** Todos los días.   **c.** Hoy.

2. _____   **a.** Mientras.   **b.** Ya no.   **c.** Ahora.

3. _____   **a.** Después de comer.   **b.** Casi nunca.   **c.** Todavía.

4. _____   **a.** Siempre.   **b.** A menudo.   **c.** Pronto.

◀)) **6.17** **Una noche en casa** Listen as Roberta describes a typical evening at home. Then decide the order
2-24 in which the following activities occur.

_____ **a.** La familia cena.

_____ **b.** Roberta y su esposo acuestan a los niños.

_____ **c.** Roberta se baña.

_____ **d.** Su esposo baña a los niños.

_____ **e.** Roberta se cepilla los dientes.

_____ **f.** Roberta lee con sus hijos.

Pronunciación 1: La *y* y la *ll*

◀)) Most Spanish speakers pronounce both **y** and **ll** the same, although there are some regional variations. It
2-25 is most common to pronounce them either like the *y* in *yes* or the *j* in *jump;* however, Argentineans and
Uruguayans pronounce them like the *z* in *azure.*

Also, some native speakers may pronounce both the **y** and the **ll** as the English *j* if it is at the beginning of the
word, but a lot softer if it is not at the beginning (like the English *y*).

Listen to the different pronunciations of the following sentence.

Yolanda y yo llegamos a la capilla por la calle Mayor.

Listen to the pronunciation of the following words and then repeat them.

llamar	llorar	lluvia	Sevilla	amarillo	valle
yo	yuca	yak	bluyines	Goya	coyote

¡Hora de reciclar! 1

6.18 **El presente progresivo** Read the descriptions of how these people feel. Then complete each
sentence with the present progressive, using a verb from the list. Use each verb only once.

ayudar   comer   dormir   escuchar   leer   salir   trabajar   viajar

1. El profesor está frustrado. Está hablando pero los estudiantes no _____ lo que dice.

2. Estoy triste. Mis padres _____ por Europa sin mí.

3. Tú estás sano; (tú) _____ bien y _____ ocho horas cada noche.

4. Ustedes están muy ocupadas; _____ largas horas en la oficina.

5. Miguel está celoso porque su exnovia _____ con otro chico.

6. Mis amigos están sorprendidos; yo _____ libros en español.

7. Mi mamá está contenta. Mi hermano y yo _____ a poner la mesa.

6.19 **¿Somos o estamos?** Combine the words or phrases to create complete sentences. You will have to decide if you need **ser** or **estar** and then conjugate it into the proper form. ¡OJO! Adjectives will need to agree with the subject.

1. mi familia / pequeño _____

2. yo / inteligente _____

3. nosotros / enamorado _____

4. mi amigo / cansado _____

5. la profesora / de España _____

6. el estudiante / en su clase _____

7. los niños / corriendo _____

¡Hora de escribir!

You are always tired at work. Write an e-mail to a co-worker explaining why you are so tired.

Paso 1 Jot down some ideas to incorporate into your e-mail. Think about the following: What time do you go to bed at night? What time do you get up in the morning? What do you do to get ready in the morning? In the morning, do you leave the house early or late? What do you do when you get to work?

© Photos To Go

Paso 2 Write an e-mail using the information you generated in **Paso 1**.

Paso 3 Edit your e-mail:

1. Is your e-mail logically organized or do you skip from one idea to the next?
2. Are there any short sentences you can combine by using **y** or **pero**?
3. Are there any spelling errors?
4. Do verbs agree with the subject?
5. Did you use the correct forms of the reflexive verbs?

_____
_____
_____
_____
_____
_____
_____
_____

Prueba tu vocabulario 2

6.20 **Definiciones** Read each of the descriptions. Write all the sports or pieces of equipment from the list below to which the description could apply.

bucear	el bádminton	el básquetbol	el béisbol	el fútbol
el fútbol americano	el golf	el tenis	el voleibol	esquiar en tabla
la natación	la pelota	la red	patinar en hielo	pescar

1. Se necesita una raqueta para jugarlo. _____

2. Se necesita una cancha para jugarlo. _____

3. Es un deporte que juegan solo dos equipos de una o dos personas. _____

4. Son dos deportes que se practican en el invierno _____

5. Es parte del equipo que se necesita para jugar voleibol. _____

6. Son deportes que se practican en el agua. _____

7. Se necesita un campo para jugarlos. _____

6.21 **¿Quién hace qué?** The following items belong to Alfonso's friends. Complete the sentences using the verbs listed below to tell what each of Alfonso's friends does on the weekend.

acampar	bucear	ir de excursión
jugar	pescar	practicar

Modelo *José juega al voleibol.*

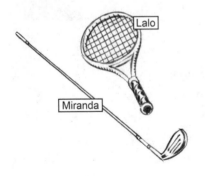
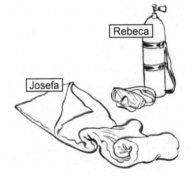
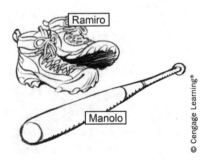

1. Lalo _____.

2. Miranda _____.

3. Josefa _____.

4. Rebeca _____.

5. Ramiro _____.

6. Manolo _____.

© Cengage Learning®

6.22 **Los pasatiempos** Read the sentences carefully and choose the most logical conclusion.

1. Juan y Ramón preparan sus sacos de dormir. Ellos...
   a. van a pescar.
   b. van a acampar.
   c. van a montar a caballo.

2. Rosa y Ana compran raquetas. Ellas quieren...
   a. pescar.
   b. patinar en hielo.
   c. practicar bádminton.

3. Lorena va al océano. Ella está aprendiendo a...
   a. bucear.
   b. levantar pesas.
   c. patinar.

4. Yo soy muy aficionada a los deportes. Todos los días voy a la cancha para practicar...
   a. básquetbol.
   b. fútbol americano.
   c. béisbol.

5. Queremos ver a nuestro equipo favorito en el estadio. Vamos a comprar...
   a. una red.
   b. una pelota.
   c. unas entradas.

6.23 **Preguntas personales** Answer the questions in complete sentences.

1. ¿Qué deportes practicas?

   _____

2. ¿Qué deportes te gusta ver?

   _____

3. ¿Quién es un(a) deportista famoso(a) y qué deporte practica?

   _____

4. ¿Cuáles son tus pasatiempos favoritos?

   _____

5. ¿Qué deportes no ves nunca en la televisión?

   _____

Prueba tu gramática 3 y 4

The preterite

6.24 **De vacaciones** Manolo and Guillermo are vacationing at a fantastic resort in Panama. Find out what they have done so far by completing this postcard that Manolo sent to his brother. You will need to conjugate all verbs in the preterite. **¡OJO!** Some of the verbs are reflexive.

¡Hola, hermano!

Guillermo y yo (1.) _____ (llegar) ayer a este maravilloso complejo turístico (resort)

en Panamá. Inmediatamente Guillermo (2.) _____ (buscar) su traje de baño y (él)

(3.) _____ (bucear) en el mar. Más tarde nosotros (4.) _____

(comer) en un restaurante y después (5.) _____ (bailar) en un club. Nosotros

(6.) _____ (volver) muy tarde a nuestra habitación y (7.) _____

(acostarse) inmediatamente. Yo (8.) _____ (despertarse) temprano y

(9.) _____ (beber) un café. Guillermo (10.) _____ (levantarse) un poco

más tarde y él y yo (11.) _____ (salir) a caminar y también (12.) _____

(visitar) un parque nacional. ¡Tenemos muchos planes para los próximos días!

Un abrazo,

Manolo

6.25 **¡Qué desastre!** Sofía, Lucas, and Beto are talking about what they did last weekend. Complete the sentences with the correct preterite form of the verb in parentheses.

Sofía: El fin de semana pasado mis hijos y yo (1.) _____ (viajar) a la costa. Desafortunadamente

(2.) _____ (llover) todo el fin de semana. Nosotros (3.) _____ (visitar) un museo

local, pero no (4.) _____ (conocer) el museo más famoso de la ciudad porque estaba cerrado.

Lucas: Mis amigos y yo (5.) _____ (acampar) en las montañas. Yo (6.) _____

(comprar) la comida y mis amigos (7.) _____ (llevar) los sacos de dormir. Pero todos

(8.) _____ (olvidar – to forget) la tienda de campaña.

Beto: Mi novia y yo fuimos de excursión. Ella (9.) _____ (dejar – to leave) el mapa en casa y

(nosotros) (10.) _____ (perderse). Finalmente después de tres horas nosotros

(11.) _____ (encontrar) el coche y (12.) _____ (volver) a casa.

6.26 **El fin de semana** Roberto's mother called him on Sunday evening and asked about his weekend. Give Roberto's answers in complete affirmative sentences using the expressions in parentheses. ¡OJO! You will need to use the preterite.

    Model   ¿Nadaste?
             (la piscina) *Sí, nadé en la piscina.*

1. ¿Practicaste un deporte?

(el básquetbol) _____

2. ¿Comiste en un restaurante?

(un restaurante francés) _____

3. ¿Compraste algo *(something)*?

(una raqueta) _____

4. ¿Leíste un libro?

(una novela de ciencia ficción) _____

5. ¿Llegaste tarde a casa?

(a la una de la mañana) _____

6.27 **¿Quién lo hizo?** Write full sentences telling what the following people did during their vacations.

    Modelo   Rosa / esquiar / Bariloche   *Rosa esquió en Bariloche.*

1. Mariana / pescar / lago _____

2. Noemí / acampar / un parque nacional _____

3. Mis amigos / aprender / bucear _____

4. Mis amigos y yo / leer / un libro en español _____

5. Mi familia / comer / restaurante _____

6. ¿Tú / montar / caballo? _____

Stem-changing verbs in the preterite

6.28 **En la playa** Complete the paragraph with the correct preterite form of the verbs in parentheses. ¡OJO! Pay attention to the verbs that have a stem change in the preterite.

Felipe, David y Ernesto (1.) _____ (salir) para la playa el viernes por la mañana y

(2.) _____ (volver) ayer. El viernes David y Felipe (3.) _____ (nadar) todo el

día pero Ernesto (4.) _____ (preferir) tomar el sol. Por la noche, ellos (5.) _____

(vestirse) y (6.) _____ (comer) en un restaurante muy bueno. Ernesto (7.) _____

(pedir) pollo frito; Felipe y David (8.) _____ (pedir) pescado. El mesero (9.) _____

(servir) la comida muy rápido y les gustó mucho. El sábado ellos (10.) _____ (despertarse)

temprano para ir a la playa otra vez. David (11.) _____ (aprender) a hacer esquí acuático.

Ernesto y Felipe (12.) _____ (preferir) quedarse en la playa. Ellos (13.) _____

(jugar) al voleibol con unas chicas. ¡(14.) _____ (divertirse) mucho!

6.29 **¿Qué pasó?** Match the situation in the first column with the reason why it happened in the second column. Then write the explanation in the preterite. Follow the model.

    Modelo   Ana está muy cansada. — (no dormir) nada anoche
                No durmió nada anoche.

1. _____ Rogelio no está en casa.

    a. (morir) su abuelo

2. _____ Marcelo está feliz.

    b. (conseguir) un aumento (*raise*)

3. _____ Miranda está llorando.

    c. (dormir) demasiado

4. _____ La maestra está enojada.

    d. (repetir) la lección tres veces

5. _____ Los estudiantes van a llegar tarde.

    e. (divertirse) en la fiesta

6. _____ El presidente está contento.

    f. (preferir) salir de viaje

1. _____

2. _____

3. _____

4. _____

5. _____

6. _____

6.30 **Unas escenas** Using the verbs indicated, write two sentences about each drawing to describe what happened in each scene.

1.

dormirse / divertirse

2.

pedir / servir

3.

vestirse / preferir

1. _____

_____

2. _____

_____

3. _____

_____

6.31 **El fin de semana** Choosing from the list of verbs below, complete the story in the preterite. ¡OJO! You will use one of the verbs twice.

conseguir	divertirse	dormir	pedir	sentirse	servir	vestirse

El fin de semana pasado yo (1.) _____ entradas para ver a mi equipo favorito de fútbol.

Mi amigo Martín también es aficionado, y por eso le (2.) _____ venir conmigo y con

mi novia. Martín y yo no (3.) _____ nada la noche anterior, porque estábamos demasiado

emocionados por ver a nuestro equipo por primera vez en el estadio. El día del juego, Martín y yo

(4.) _____ con los colores de nuestro equipo. Cuando llegamos al estadio nos sentamos para

ver el partido. Mi novia tenía hambre y (5.) _____ un perro caliente. El vendedor le

(6.) _____ un perro caliente con mucha salsa picante *(spicy)*. Después de 15 minutos mi novia

(7.) _____ muy mal. ¡Ella no (8.) _____ para nada! Lo bueno fue que nuestro

equipo ganó.

¡Hora de escuchar! 2

🔊 **6.32** **Las actividades favoritas** You will hear a conversation between three friends. Listen carefully
2-26   and write who will do each activity this weekend: Dalia, Lalo, or Federico.

1. _____ acampar

2. _____ jugar al fútbol

3. _____ jugar al tenis

4. _____ jugar al voleibol

🔊 **6.33** **Ayer** You will hear six questions. Decide which of the answers below is correct and write the letter in
2-27   the blank beside the number of the question.

1. _____   **a.** Sí, gané el partido.

2. _____   **b.** Después regresó a la casa.

3. _____   **c.** Jugué al fútbol.

4. _____   **d.** Después salí a comer con el equipo.

5. _____   **e.** No, perdió el partido.

6. _____   **f.** Jugó al béisbol.

🔊 **6.34** **El fin de semana** You will hear the story of what Olga did on Saturday. Listen to it and then
2-28   decide if the statements are true (**cierto**) or false (**falso**).

1. Cierto   Falso   Llovió el sábado.

2. Cierto   Falso   Planearon jugar al fútbol en un club deportivo.

3. Cierto   Falso   Todos miraron un video en casa de Andrés.

4. Cierto   Falso   Maritza tuvo (had) un pequeño accidente.

5. Cierto   Falso   Andrés preparó comida para sus amigos.

Pronunciación 2: La z

🔊 In Spanish, the letter **z** is pronounced like the *s* in the English word *sun*. Listen to the pronunciation of the
2-29 following words.

   zapato   lápiz   empezar   izquierda   arroz

However, in Spain the letter **z** as well as the soft **c** (**ci** and **ce** combinations), are pronounced similarly to the *th*
in the English word *thin*. Listen to the pronunciation of the following words.

   almuerzo   cinco   cenar   luz   conocer   lección

🔊 **Trabalenguas** Practice the pronunciation of the letter **z** with the following tongue twister:
2-30
   Rosa Rizo reza en ruso,

   en ruso reza Rosa Rizo.

¡Hora de reciclar! 2

6.35 **Los verbos irregulares en la primera persona** Complete the paragraph with the correct
form of the appropriate verb in the present tense.

Yo no (1.) _____ (oír/dar) el despertador y cuando por fin me despierto, (2.) _____

(venir/ver) que ya son las ocho. No (3.) _____ (poner/hacer) la cama porque no tengo tiempo.

Me visto rápidamente y (4.) _____ (salir/ganar) para la oficina. (5.) _____ (Traer/

Conducir) muy rápido y, desafortunadamente, me para *(stops)* un policía. Como estoy muy nervioso, no le

(6.) _____ (decir/conocer) nada. Sin embargo *(Nevertheless),* el policía tiene compasión y no me

(7.) _____ (seguir/dar) una multa *(fine).* (8.) _____ (Seguir/Decir) hacia *(to)* la oficina

y estoy un poco más tranquilo, pero cuando llego a la oficina, me doy cuenta *(I realize)* de que yo no

(9.) _____ (traer/volver) el reporte que mi jefa necesita. Está enojada y ahora ella

(10.) _____ (conducir/venir) a regañarme *(reprimand me).* ¡Qué mañana!

6.36 **¿Saber o conocer?** Decide if you need **saber** or **conocer** and then conjugate it correctly in the
present tense.

1. El dependiente _____ dónde están las raquetas.

2. Mis amigos y yo _____ patinar en hielo.

3. Yo _____ a un deportista famoso.

4. El agente _____ cuánto cuesta la entrada.

5. Los deportistas _____ jugar al tenis.

6. ¿Tú _____ el Estadio Azteca?

CAPÍTULO 7 ¿Qué te gusta comer?

Prueba tu vocabulario 1

7.1 **Las compras** You are hosting a special dinner and have to make a shopping list. You've been given the name of each dish and the first letter of the ingredients you need to buy. **¡OJO!** Some of the items are plural!

Entremés: Guacamole: aguacate, c __ __ __ __ __ __ , t __ __ __ __ __

Plato principal: Tortilla española: h __ __ __ __ __ , p __ __ __ __ , a __ __ __ __ __

Postre: Ensalada de frutas: p __ __ __ , u __ __ __ , m __ __ __ __ __ __ __ ,

p __ __ __ __ __ __ __ , m __ __ __ __ , n __ __ __ __ __ __ __

7.2 **¿Cuál no pertenece?** For each group of words, write the one that does not belong.

Modelo papa, zanahoria, naranja, pepinillo _____*pepinillo*_____

1. tomate, fresa, manzana, lechuga _____

2. yogur, piña, mantequilla, queso _____

3. jamón, maíz, pan, mostaza _____

4. pepino, brócoli, zanahoria, catsup _____

5. durazno, cereal, uvas, piña _____

6. sandía, catsup, mostaza, mayonesa _____

7.3 **¿Qué es?** Read the descriptions and indicate the letter of the item that best completes each sentence.

1. Generalmente comemos _____ en el desayuno.
   a. zanahorias   **b.** huevos   **c.** pepinillos

2. _____ es una fruta tropical que se cultiva en Costa Rica.
   a. La leche   **b.** El durazno   **c.** La piña

3. Me gusta poner fruta en mi _____ .
   a. yogur   **b.** queso   **c.** papa

4. Un ingrediente importante de un sándwich es _____ .
   a. la leche   **b.** el pepino   **c.** el pan

5. Soy vegetariano y por eso nunca como _____ .
   a. jamón   **b.** rebanadas   **c.** catsup

6. El queso es a la pizza lo que la leche es _____ .
   a. al maíz   **b.** a la crema   **c.** al cereal

7.4 **¿Cuánto cuesta?** Write out the numbers to tell how much the following items cost in Colombian pesos.

1. 1 kilo de queso $6.950 _____ pesos

2. una docena de huevos $3.725 _____ pesos

3. 2 kilos de jamón $11.200 _____ pesos

4. 1.5 kilos de manzanas $5.175 _____ pesos

5. dos litros de leche $8.515 _____ pesos

7.5 **Asociaciones** Match an item in column **A** with an item in column **B**, and explain the relationship between them.

Modelo la catsup—las papas fritas
Ponemos catsup en las papas fritas.

A   **B**

1. la leche   **a.** la mantequilla

2. la rebanada   **b.** el cereal

3. las fresas   **c.** el pepinillo

4. las papas   **d.** las zanahorias

5. el pepino   **e.** las uvas

6. la mermelada   **f.** el pan

1. _____

2. _____

3. _____

4. _____

5. _____

6. _____

Prueba tu gramática 1 y 2

Irregular verbs in the preterite

7.6 **La cena** Tania invited a few friends to dinner, so she went to the supermarket to get some ingredients to cook. Complete her story with the past tense of the verbs in parentheses.

Yo (1.) _____ (hacer) una lista de todos los ingredientes necesarios para hacer una gran

cena para mis amigos. (2.) _____ (Conducir) mi auto al supermercado. Cuando llegué no

(3.) _____ (ver) ninguna fruta ni verdura. Le pregunté a un dependiente y él

(4.) _____ (decir) que hay un rumor de que los precios de todas las frutas van a subir *(to go up)*.

Por eso muchas personas (5.) _____ (venir) al supermercado. ¡(Yo) no (6.) _____

(poder) comprar muchos de los ingredientes! Al final, (7.) _____ (tener) que comprar una pizza

para mis amigos. Afortunadamente ellos (8.) _____ (traer) un postre *(dessert)* y una tortilla

española.

7.7 **Los cuentos de hadas** Decide which characters did the following things. Then complete the sentences, conjugating the verbs in the preterite.

andar por el bosque *(woods)* con su padre   traerle comida a su abuelita
poder despertar a la Bella Durmiente con un beso   ponerse zapatos de cristal
saber que alguien estaba *(was)* en su casa   querer ser la más bella de todas

1. Los tres osos *(bears)* _____.

2. La madrastra de Blancanieves _____.

3. El príncipe _____.

4. Hansel y Gretel _____.

5. Caperucita Roja *(Little Red Riding Hood)* _____.

6. La Cenicienta *(Cinderella)* _____.

7.8 **Preguntas** Martín and his wife Cecilia are having guests over for dinner. Cecilia asks Martín whether he did what she needed him to do. Complete her questions with the **tú** form of the verb in parentheses. **¡OJO!** You don't need to include the word **tú** in your answers.

1. ¿_____ (Ir) al supermercado?

2. ¿_____ (Poder) encontrar queso?

3. ¿_____ (Traer) cebollas también?

4. ¿_____ (Poner) las verduras en el refrigerador?

5. ¿_____ (Hacer) la ensalada?

7.9 **En la granja** Mariana went to an organic farm to get some fresh fruit. Complete the story with the preterite of the most logical verb from the list. You will need to repeat one.

conducir	dar	decir	hacer	ir	pedir	ponerse	tener

Mariana (1.) _____ a una granja orgánica para comprar fruta fresca. Primero ella

(2.) _____ una cita (appointment). El dueño de la granja (3.) _____ "¡Claro que

puede venir! Usted misma puede recoger (pick) la fruta". Entonces Mariana (4.) _____ sus

bluyines y (5.) _____ su auto a la granja. Ella (6.) _____ que manejar por una

hora. Mariana compró cinco kilos de uvas, cinco kilos de duraznos y tres kilos de manzanas porque su amiga

Florencia le (7.) _____ comprar fruta para ella también. Florencia (8.) _____ un

pay (pie) de durazno y le (9.) _____ la mitad a Mariana. ¡No hay nada como comer fruta fresca!

7.10 **¡Qué restaurante más raro!** Meche and Juan Carlos went to a restaurant, and they had an unusual experience. Complete the paragraph with the preterite of the verbs in parentheses to find out what happened.

Meche y Juan Carlos (1.) _____ (pedir) fruta fresca, pero el mesero (2.) _____

(traer) fruta de lata (can). Meche (3.) _____ (ver) sopa de brócoli en el menú—¡su favorita! Ella

(4.) _____ (querer) pedir la sopa, pero el mesero (5.) _____ (decir) que

no la recomendaba. El mesero (6.) _____ (ir) a la cocina por agua, pero cuando

(7.) _____ (venir) a la mesa de Juan Carlos y Meche (8.) _____ (poner) el agua

debajo de la mesa. Meche y Juan Carlos (9.) _____ (ver) que debajo de la mesa había un gatito.

Ellos descubrieron que el mesero le (10.) _____ (dar) el agua al gatito, no a ellos. Después de

todo, ¡no (11.) _____ (ser) tan mala su experiencia en el restaurante!

Por and para and prepositional pronouns

7.11 **La cosecha** Complete the story using **por** or **para**.

El año pasado decidí plantar verduras en mi jardín (1.) _____ ahorrar dinero. Fui a una tienda

especializada y compré semillas (seeds) (2.) _____ plantar. Estuve en la tienda

(3.) _____ una hora y media, pero no encontré todo lo necesario. (4.) _____ eso tuve

que ir a otra tienda. Finalmente regresé a casa. Mi amigo Juan vino (5.) _____ ayudarme a plantar

las semillas. Trabajamos (6.) _____ varios días. Planté lechugas, zanahorias, pepinos y tomates

(7.) _____ hacer ensaladas en el verano. Cuando las plantas crecieron, una familia de mapaches

(raccoons) comenzó a venir (8.) _____ las noches (9.) _____ comer... Este año voy a

comprar mis verduras en el mercado.

7.12 **Frutas y verduras** Decide if you need **por** or **para** to complete the ideas.

1. _____ supuesto quiero estar sano y _____ eso como muchas frutas y verduras.

2. Voy al supermercado _____ uvas, piña y sandía _____ hacer una ensalada de frutas

   _____ el almuerzo.

3. Mientras voy _____ el supermercado, paso _____ la casa de una amiga

   _____ pedirle un favor.

4. _____ fin llego a casa, hago mi ensalada de frutas y llamo a mis amigos _____

   teléfono _____ invitarlos a almorzar conmigo.

7.13 **Oraciones incompletas** Complete the following sentences in a logical manner.

1. Yo fui a la cocina para _____.

2. Compré una docena de huevos por _____.

3. Corté unas papas para _____.

4. Quise hornear un pastel *(cake)* para _____.

5. Estuvimos en el restaurante por _____.

7.14 **Combinaciones** Use the elements below to form complete sentences using the preterite tense. For each item, choose **por** or **para** as needed.

   Modelo (yo) / ir al restaurante / (por/para) / cenar
   Fui al restaurante para cenar.

1. el chef / comprar / jamón / (por/para) / hacer un sándwich

   _____

2. la mesera / traer / pan / (por/para) / los clientes

   _____

3. el granjero *(farmer)* / trabajar / (por/para) / varios meses

   _____

4. los cocineros / comprar / piñas / (por/para) / cien pesos

   _____

5. (yo) no poder / hacer una ensalada / (por/para) / no tener / lechuga

   _____

7.15 **Unos regalos** Complete this conversation with the correct prepositional pronouns. **¡OJO!** You may have to use **conmigo** or **contigo**.

Flora: Este verano fui de viaje a Puerto Rico. No fui sola; mi esposo fue (1.) _____, pero nuestra

hija no pudo ir con (2.) _____. Entonces, compramos una tarjeta postal y un regalo para

(3.) _____.

Delia: ¿Y qué te compraste?

Flora: Yo nada, pero mi esposo es muy generoso y compró un vestido para (4.) _____ y esta

camiseta para (5.) _____ *(you)*.

Delia: ¡Qué bueno! ¿Y compraste algo para tu esposo?

Flora: ¡Por supuesto! Compré una guayabera para (6.) _____.

¡Hora de escuchar! 1

🔊 **7.16** **¿De quién es la bolsa?** You will hear a description of the items that Lola, Miguel, Alfredo, and
2-31 José Luis bought. Listen to the descriptions, and write the name of the owner of each bag of groceries on the line below the bag. **¡OJO!** One drawing will not be used; write an X in that blank.

1.

_____

2.

_____

3.

_____

4.

_____

5.

_____

© Cengage Learning®

🔊 **7.17** **¿Cuál es?** Listen carefully to what the speakers say and decide which one of the items
2-32　　　　they are referring to.

1. _____　　a. el pepino　　　　b. la manzana　　　　c. la lechuga

2. _____　　a. el cereal　　　　b. los huevos　　　　c. la leche

3. _____　　a. la mostaza　　　　b. el pan　　　　　　c. la mermelada

4. _____　　a. el tomate　　　　b. el plátano　　　　c. el yogur

5. _____　　a. el queso　　　　b. la mantequilla　　c. la papa

🔊 **7.18** **La ropa vieja** Listen to the conversation between a couple and answer the questions below.
2-33

1. ¿Qué es la ropa vieja? _____

2. ¿Qué ingredientes tiene? _____

3. ¿Con qué se sirve? _____

4. ¿Qué necesita comprar la señora? _____

5. ¿Y qué quiere el señor? _____

¡Hora de reciclar! 1

7.19 **El pretérito 1** Complete the paragraph using the necessary form of the verbs in the preterite.

Ayer yo (1.) _____ (ir) al supermercado con mi hijo. Nosotros (2.) _____ (llegar) a la

sección de las verduras primero, y yo (3.) _____ (buscar) algunas frutas frescas. Luego nosotros

(4.) _____ (pasar) por el pasillo de los cereales. Yo (5.) _____ (escoger) un cereal

nutritivo. Mi hijo (6.) _____ (pedir) que le comprara Choco Pops y yo le (7.) _____

(decir) que no porque tienen mucha azúcar *(sugar)*. Entonces él (8.) _____ (empezar) a llorar y

gritar. Las otras personas en el supermercado me (9.) _____ (mirar). Al final nosotros

(10.) _____ (tener) que salir del supermercado sin comprar nada.

7.20 **Los reflexivos** Complete each sentence with the correct form of the appropriate verb in the present tense. ¡OJO! Not all the sentences take reflexive verbs. You may use each verb only once.

acostar(se)   dormir(se)   maquillar(se)
afeitar(se)   estirarse   quitar(se)
bañar(se)   levantar(se) sentar(se)

1. El señor Rodríguez _____ la cara.

2. Después de correr, necesito _____.

3. Pero ¿por qué _____ los ojos, Lola? ¡Vamos a nadar en la piscina!

4. Si ustedes no _____ al menos seis horas cada noche, van a _____ durante la clase por la mañana.

5. Tenemos que _____ al perro. Huele *(He smells)* muy mal.

6. A las ocho de la noche, la señora Vélez _____ a su hijo en su cama y luego ella _____ en la sala para ver su programa favorito.

7. Los sábados mi esposo y yo _____ temprano porque el mercado abre a las nueve.

8. Cuando llega del trabajo, mi papá no ve la hora de *(can't wait)* _____ los zapatos.

¡Hora de escribir!

You are writing a blog and sharing some of your experiences. Write a paragraph about a special dish.

Paso 1 Think of a special dish you'd like to write about. It might be something you eat on a special occasion or on a holiday, a family recipe or something you enjoy preparing. Jot down as many things about the dish as you can. Think about the following questions: Why is it special to you? Where or who is the recipe from? When do you serve it? What ingredients do you need?

Paso 2 Write a topic sentence in which you introduce your special dish to your reader. Develop the remainder of the paragraph using the idea you generated in **Paso 1.**

Paso 3 Conclude your paragraph with a serving suggestion. How should it be served or what should it be served with?

Paso 4 Edit your paragraph:

1. Do all of your sentences in your first paragraph support the topic sentence?
2. Do you have smooth transitions?
3. Do verbs agree with the subject?

© Blend Images/Shutterstock

Prueba tu vocabulario 2

7.21 **Los utensilios** Match the dishes with the utensils needed to serve or eat each item.

1. _____ la limonada

2. _____ la sopa de verduras

3. _____ el vino

4. _____ una ensalada

5. _____ el café

a. una taza

b. una copa

c. un vaso

d. una cuchara

e. un tenedor

7.22 **El menú** Place the food items under the appropriate menu categories.

té	vino	jugo	totopos
café	flan	helado	enchiladas
quesadillas	cerdo asado	carne asada	coctel de camarones
pavo al horno	sopa de tomate	pastel de vainilla	

entremeses

_____

_____

_____

_____

postres

_____

_____

_____

_____

platos principales

_____

_____

_____

_____

bebidas

_____

_____

_____

_____

7.23 **En la cocina** Jimena is having a big family dinner and has a lot to remember. Using logic and the following vocabulary words, complete her ideas.

camarones   refrescos   fruta   cucharas   azúcar   vino   cerveza

A ver… mi abuela quiere su café con mucha (1.) _____. Mi abuelo no quiere café; él

desea una (2.) _____ muy fría porque hace calor. De postre, mi sobrina Luci prefiere

comer (3.) _____ y no helado porque está a dieta. Mi esposo Ramón es alérgico a los

mariscos *(shellfish)*, así que a él no le debo servir (4.) _____. A mi primo Manolo le

gusta el (5.) _____, así que necesito poner una copa para él. Los niños siempre quieren

beber (6.) _____ porque no les gustan el agua ni los jugos. ¡Ah! Y no debo olvidar traer

(7.) _____ para todos, para tomar la sopa.

Prueba tu gramática 3 y 4

Direct object pronouns 1

7.24 **¿Cómo lo quiere?** A waitress is serving a couple, but is unsure as to how to serve the items they have ordered. Complete the couple's answers using the direct object pronouns **lo, la, los,** or **las.**

Modelo   ¿Cómo quiere la carne?
_La_ quiero asada.

1. ¿Cómo desea sus papas?   _____ quiero fritas.

2. ¿De qué sabor quiere su helado?   _____ quiero de chocolate.

3. ¿Cómo quieren sus cervezas?   _____ queremos muy frías.

4. ¿Cómo desea usted su sopa?   _____ quiero muy caliente.

5. ¿Ustedes prefieren el pastel grande o el chico?   ¡_____ preferimos muy grande!

6. ¿Y prefieren la cuenta ahora o después?   _____ preferimos después.

7.25 **¿Qué tomas?** Rewrite the second sentence in each pair using the correct direct object pronoun in order to avoid unnecessary repetition.

Modelo   Yo como muchas zanahorias. Pongo zanahorias en mi ensalada.
Las pongo en mi ensalada.

1. Mi padre prefiere el café. Toma el café con el desayuno.

   _____

2. Me gustan los jugos. Por eso tomo los jugos todas las mañanas.

   _____

3. A mi hermanita le gusta la leche. Siempre pide la leche por la mañana.

   _____

4. Mi madre compra mucho té. Ella prefiere tomar el té después de comer.

   _____

5. Hay una variedad de bebidas en casa. Todos estamos tomando las bebidas.

   _____

6. El helado es un buen postre. Por eso siempre compro helado cuando voy al supermercado.

   _____

7.26 **¿Qué hacemos con esto (this)?** Match each item with a logical verb. Then use direct object pronouns to write a short sentence telling what we do with each item.

> **Modelo**   la carne—cortar
> *La cortamos.*

1. _____ las cervezas   **a.** comer en los cumpleaños

2. _____ el mantel   **b.** poner en la comida

3. _____ la sal   **c.** leer

4. _____ el pastel   **d.** poner sobre la mesa

5. _____ los menús   **e.** beber

6. _____ la cena   **f.** cocinar

7.27 **Preguntas personales** Answer the questions in complete sentences. Be sure to use direct object pronouns.

> **Modelo**   ¿Cómo prefieres el pollo: frito o asado?
> *Lo prefiero asado.*

1. ¿Dónde prefieres comprar la comida?

   _____

2. ¿Con qué frecuencia tomas café?

   _____

3. ¿Comes verduras todos los días?

   _____

4. ¿Quién pone la mesa antes de comer?

   _____

5. ¿Cuándo tomas refrescos?

   _____

Direct object pronouns 2

7.28 **Traducciones** Choose the correct translation and write the letter in the blank.

1. _____ ¿Me invitas a cenar?   **a.** Shall I call you after work?

2. _____ ¿Te invito a cenar?   **b.** Will you help me fix dinner?

3. _____ ¿Me ayudas a preparar la cena? **c.** Will you invite me to dinner?

4. _____ ¿Te ayudo a preparar la cena?   **d.** Shall I help you fix dinner?

5. _____ ¿Me llamas después de trabajar? **e.** Shall I invite you to dinner?

6. _____ ¿Te llamo después de trabajar? **f.** Will you call me after work?

7.29 Tu mejor amigo Answer the following questions in complete sentences.

Modelo   ¿Tu mejor amigo te escucha?
Sí, *mi mejor amigo me escucha.*

1. ¿Tu mejor amigo te invita a salir?

Sí, _____.

2. ¿Tu mejor amigo te llama mucho por teléfono?

No, _____.

3. ¿Tu mejor amigo te comprende?

Sí, _____.

4. ¿Tu mejor amigo te escucha cuando tienes problemas?

Sí, _____.

5. ¿Tu mejor amigo te ayuda con la tarea?

No, _____.

7.30 Una evaluación The university is conducting instructor evaluations. Complete the conversation with one of the following direct object pronouns: **me** or **nos**.

DIRECTOR: ¿El profesor los ayuda a ustedes?

ESTUDIANTE: Sí, (1.) _____ ayuda mucho.

DIRECTOR: ¿Y él los escucha cuando tienen preguntas?

ESTUDIANTE: Sí, siempre (2.) _____ escucha.

DIRECTOR: ¿Él los trata (treat) con respeto a todos ustedes?

ESTUDIANTE: Sí, (3.) _____ trata con respeto.

DIRECTOR: ¿Él te llama a tu casa?

ESTUDIANTE: No, no (4.) _____ llama a mi casa.

DIRECTOR: ¿Él te visita?

ESTUDIANTE: No, no (5.) _____ visita.

DIRECTOR: Bueno, muchas gracias por tu tiempo.

7.31 **¿Quién?** Answer the questions, using the information in parentheses and the correct direct object pronouns to replace the underlined words.

Modelo   ¿Quién <u>te</u> llama por la noche? (mis padres)
Mis padres me llaman por la noche.

1. ¿Quién los ayuda <u>a ustedes</u> con la tarea? (un tutor)

_____

2. ¿Quién <u>te</u> invita a salir los fines de semana? (mis amigos)

_____

3. ¿Quién los escucha <u>a ustedes</u> en la clase? (la profesora)

_____

4. ¿Quién <u>te</u> lleva a la universidad? (mi compañero de clase)

_____

5. ¿Quién <u>te</u> visita con frecuencia? (mi familia)

_____

¡Hora de escuchar! 2

7.32 **Las definiciones** You will hear six definitions. Write the vocabulary words that they describe.

You will hear: Es blanca y la usamos para darle más sabor a la comida.
You will write: *la sal*

1. _____

2. _____

3. _____

4. _____

5. _____

6. _____

🔊 **7.33** **¿Qué es?** You will hear several descriptions of food items. Listen carefully and think logically,
2-35   paying attention to the object pronouns, and choose the item to which they refer.

You will hear: Las como fritas, con mucha sal y catsup.

You will write: _las papas_   los tomates   las papas   el arroz   la fruta

1. _____ el vino   los camarones   la hamburguesa   las papas fritas

2. _____ el cuchillo   los platos   la servilleta   las tazas

3. _____ el vino   los refrescos   la cerveza   las limonadas

4. _____ el pescado   los entremeses   la sopa   las verduras

5. _____ el té   los cuchillos   la leche   las cucharas

6. _____ el pan   los tomates   la carne   las enchiladas

🔊 **7.34** **Problemas en el restaurante** Rosa is eating in a restaurant, but things are not going well.
2-36   Listen to the conversation between her and the waiter, and decide whether the statements below are
true (**cierto**) or false (**falso**). Rewrite the false statements, correcting the errors.

1. Cierto   Falso   Rosa pide el pollo asado.

_____

2. Cierto   Falso   Rosa pide una cerveza para tomar.

_____

3. Cierto   Falso   Rosa necesita una cuchara.

_____

4. Cierto   Falso   La comida de Rosa está fría.

_____

5. Cierto   Falso   El tenedor no está limpio (clean).

_____

¡Hora de reciclar! 2

7.35 **El pretérito 2** Piedad wrote this e-mail to her friend. Complete the message with the correct preterite form of the verb in parentheses.

Querida Ana Milena:

¿Cómo estás, amiga? ¿(1.) _____ (Leer, tú) el mensaje que yo te

(2.) _____ (mandar) el jueves? Te (3.) _____ (escribir) para

decirte que (yo) (4.) _____ (llegar) bien a Montevideo. Bueno, el jueves Armando

y yo estábamos *(were)* tan cansados que (5.) _____ (comer) en un restaurante

y (6.) _____ (volver) al hotel. Pero el viernes yo (7.) _____

(levantarse) temprano y (8.) _____ (conocer) la ciudad un poco. Luego Armando

y yo (9.) _____ (montar) a caballo en la playa. Fue increíble. Mañana vamos a un

espectáculo de bailes folklóricos. Tienes que escribirme para contarme sobre la semana pasada.

¿(10.) _____ (Acampar) tú y Alberto en las montañas, o (11.) _____

(jugar) él en el torneo de tenis?

Un abrazo de tu amiga,

Piedad

7.36 **Las expresiones de tiempo y frecuencia** Luisa habla de una cena que prepara para sus amigos. Completa las oraciones con la expresión de tiempo o frecuencia apropiada.

antes (de) **después (de)** **mientras** **nunca** **siempre** **todavía** **vez**

1. Una _____ al mes invito a mis amigos a mi casa a comer.

2. Mañana van a venir y _____ no sé qué voy a preparar.

3. Silvia no come carne, y por eso _____ sirvo un plato vegetariano cuando ella viene.

4. Voy a ofrecer vino y queso _____ servir la cena y _____ la cena quiero

servir un postre.

5. Bueno, _____ conduzco al supermercado, voy a pensar más en mi menú.

CAPÍTULO 8 ¿Qué haces dentro y fuera de la casa?

Prueba tu vocabulario 1

8.1 **Un día para limpiar** Circle the most logical answer.

¡Tenemos mucho que hacer en la casa! Yo debo (1.) (regar / trapear / planchar) la ropa, pero primero tengo que (2.) (guardar / cortar / ordenar) el césped. Mi esposo tiene que (3.) (hacer / sacudir / lavar) las camas. Después, nosotros vamos al supermercado para comprar un nuevo (4.) (trapeador / tabla de planchar / bote de basura) porque el nuestro se rompió cuando limpiaba el piso. También necesitamos una nueva (5.) (escoba / plancha / manguera) para barrer el piso. Finalmente, mi hija prometió que va a (6.) (sacudir / secar / regar) los muebles de la sala… ¡menos mal que todos ayudamos a limpiar!

8.2 **¿Qué palabra es?** Complete the sentences with vocabulary words.

    Modelo Debes C _O_ _L_ _G_ _A_ _R_ la ropa en el armario.

1. Antes de servir la cena, debemos P __ __ __ __ la M __ __ __.

2. Para planchar, necesitamos una tabla de planchar y una P __ __ __ __ __ __.

3. Después de levantarnos, debemos H __ __ __ __ la C __ __ __.

4. La A __ __ __ __ __ __ __ __ __ es un aparato electrodoméstico que usamos para limpiar la alfombra.

5. Si no sirve un aparato, y no es posible repararlo, debemos tirarlo en la B __ __ __ __ __.

8.3 **Las descripciones** Match the descriptions with the chores or household objects.

1. _____ poner la mesa   **a.** La uso para regar.

2. _____ el cortacésped   **b.** La uso para barrer.

3. _____ la escoba   **c.** Lo hacemos después de lavar los platos.

4. _____ secar   **d.** Lo necesitamos para hacer un quehacer del jardín.

5. _____ la manguera   **e.** Lo hacemos después de comer.

6. _____ recoger la mesa   **f.** Lo hacemos antes de comer.

Prueba tu gramática 1 y 2

The imperfect

8.4 **En esos tiempos** Doña María is 80 years old and she is talking about the chores she used to do when she was a child. Complete her description with the imperfect form of the appropriate verb in parentheses.

Cuando yo (1.) _____ (estar / ser) niña, mis padres (2.) _____ (ser / estar) muy estrictos.

Ellos (3.) _____ (querer / saber) ver nuestra casa siempre limpia. Yo (4.) _____ (pasar /

barrer) la aspiradora una vez a la semana. Mi hermana mayor (5.) _____ (cortar / sacudir) la sala

todos los días. Todos nosotros (6.) _____ (regar / hacer) nuestras camas temprano por la mañana,

antes de ir a la escuela. Mi hermanita (7.) _____ (poner / recoger) la mesa después de comer, y yo

(8.) _____ (guardar / lavar) los platos mientras mi hermano los (9.) _____ (planchar /

secar). La verdad es que mis padres criaron *(raised)* a unos hijos muy trabajadores y responsables.

8.5 **Los quehaceres** While growing up, everyone in Lucila's house had chores to do. Complete her sentences using the imperfect to tell what everyone had to do.

1. Yo (poner) _____ la mesa antes de comer y después (recoger) _____ los platos.

2. Mis hermanos (limpiar) _____ los baños.

3. Mi hermana y yo (lavar) _____ y (secar) _____ los platos.

4. Mi padre (cortar) _____ el césped.

5. Mi madre (sacudir) _____ la sala y el comedor.

6. Todos nosotros (hacer) _____ nuestras camas.

8.6 **Mi compañera de casa** Complete the following story with the indicated verbs in the imperfect.

Cuando yo (1.) _____ (asistir) a la universidad yo (2.) _____ (vivir) con Mayra, una

chica un poco extraña. A ella (3.) _____ (gustarle) cocinar y limpiar... ¡ella (4.) _____

(ser) la compañera de casa ideal! Un día encontramos un perrito afuera de nuestro apartamento.

¡(5.) _____ (ser) muy mono *(cute)*! Decidimos adoptarlo. Yo (6.) _____ (llevar) al

perrito a caminar todos los días y también le (7.) _____ (servir) su comida. En realidad Mayra

no (8.) _____ (tener) responsabilidades con el perrito, pero ella (9.) _____ (estar)

obsesionada con tener la casa y el perro limpio. ¡Ella (10.) _____ (bañar) al perro todos los días!

El pobre perrito (11.) _____ (correr) cuando él (12.) _____ (ver) a Mayra. A final de

ese año Mayra terminó sus estudios y se fue a vivir a otra ciudad. Yo la (13.) _____ (extrañar *to

miss)* mucho ¡pero al perrito le (14.) _____ (alegrar) no bañarse todos los días!

8.7 **De adolescente** Choose two of the following people, and write three sentences for each in which you describe what their high school years were like. Tell what they used to be like, what they used to do, and how others reacted to them.

Manuel

Olga

Fabiana

Fernando

© Cengage Learning®

1. _____

_____

_____

2. _____

_____

_____

Indefinite and negative expressions

8.8 **La palabra lógica** Complete the ideas with the appropriate word.

1. No me gusta planchar (ninguna / nada / ningún).

2. ¡Tengo que limpiar toda la casa pero (nada / nadie / algo) me ayuda a limpiar!

3. ¿Tienes (algún / alguna / algo) trapo? Necesito sacudir la sala.

4. Mis hijos deben ordenar sus dormitorios pero (ninguno / tampoco / ni) tiene tiempo.

5. ¿Hay (alguno / alguna / alguien) escoba para barrer la cocina?

6. No quiero hacer mi cama hoy (tampoco / ni / nada) mañana.

_____

8.9 **¡Qué negativo!** Rafael and Franco live together. Rafael is a bit negative. Complete their conversation with the appropriate negative expression.

Franco: Nuestra casa es un desastre, pero no quiero limpiarla hoy. ¿Y tú?

Rafael: No, no quiero limpiar (1.) _____.

Franco: ¿Qué vas a hacer ahora?

Rafael: No voy a hacer (2.) _____.

Franco: ¿Quieres ir a la piscina o al parque?

Rafael: No quiero ir (3.) _____ a la piscina (4.) _____ al parque; hace

mucho calor.

Franco: Podemos llamar a algunos amigos para ir al cine.

Rafael: No quiero llamar a (5.) _____ amigo; no quiero salir con

(6.) _____.

Franco: ¡Ay, Rafael! (7.) _____ quieres hacer (8.) _____.

_____

8.10 **Entrevista** Mauricio is planning to move into an apartment with another student and he has some questions. Answer his questions using the negative expressions.

1. ¿Tienes una mascota?   No, _____.

2. No cocino, ¿y tú?   No, _____.

3. ¿Hay algo en el refrigerador?   No, _____.

4. ¿Necesito comprar una escoba o un trapeador?   No, _____.

5. ¿Alguien viene a limpiar el apartamento?   No, _____.

8.11 **Dos rutinas diferentes** Jorge is describing a typical Saturday to his friend, Gabriel. Gabriel doesn't do any of the things that Jorge does. Write Gabriel's statements, using negative expressions.

Modelo Riego algunas plantas en el jardín.
No riego ninguna planta en el jardín.

JORGE: Siempre hago mi cama en la mañana.

GABRIEL: (1.) _____

JORGE: Plancho algunas camisas para la semana.

GABRIEL: (2.) _____

JORGE: Salgo para comprar algo para la cena.

GABRIEL: (3.) _____

JORGE: Invito a alguien para cenar.

GABRIEL: (4.) _____

JORGE: Lavo y seco los platos antes de acostarme.

GABRIEL: (5.) _____

¡Hora de escuchar! 1

8.12 **¿Es lógico?** Listen to the statements and decide if they are logical (**lógico**) or illogical (**ilógico**).

3-2

1. lógico   ilógico

2. lógico   ilógico

3. lógico   ilógico

4. lógico   ilógico

5. lógico   ilógico

6. lógico   ilógico

8.13 **Respuestas negativas** Horacio wants to know more about his new roommate and asks him questions about when he was a child. Listen to his questions and write the number of the question in the blank beside the most logical answer. One response will not be used.

3-3

a. _____ Nada.   **c.** _____ Nadie.   **e.** _____ Nunca.

b. _____ Ninguno.   **d.** _____ Con nadie.   **f.** _____ Yo tampoco.

🔊 **8.14** **Una noche en casa** Listen as Roberta remembers a typical evening at home when she was a
3-4   child. Then decide if the following statements are true (**cierto**) or false (**falso**).

1. Cierto   Falso   Roberta se bañaba por la mañana.

2. Cierto   Falso   A Roberta no le gustaba bañarse.

3. Cierto   Falso   Su papá lavaba los platos después de cenar.

4. Cierto   Falso   Después de escuchar una historia, Roberta y su hermano miraban la tele.

¡Hora de reciclar! 1

8.15 **Los pronombres de objeto directo I** Match the vocabulary word in the first column with
the most logical verb in the second column. Then write a complete sentence telling what we do with
the items.

    Modelo   la aspiradora   pasar   *La pasamos.*

1. _____ los platos   **a.** sacar

2. _____ la ropa   **b.** cortar

3. _____ la basura   **c.** sacudir

4. _____ los muebles   **d.** barrer

5. _____ los pisos   **e.** planchar

6. _____ el césped   **f.** secar

1. _____

2. _____

3. _____

4. _____

5. _____

6. _____

8.16 **Los pronombres del objeto directo II** Complete the following conversations with the direct object pronouns **me** and **te**.

1. —¡La casa es un desastre! ¿_____ ayudas, mi amor?

   —Por supuesto. ¿Cómo _____ puedo ayudar?

   —Si tú limpias el baño, yo puedo limpiar la cocina.

2. —¿Dónde estás? No _____ veo.

   —Estoy enfrente de la tienda. ¿_____ ves ahora?

   —Sí, ahora sí.

3. —¿_____ vas a acompañar (*to accompany*) al cine?

   —Sí, y si quieres _____ invito a cenar después.

   —¡Excelente! _____ veo enfrente del cine a las 4:00.

¡Hora de escribir!

A parenting magazine has asked readers to write in and describe what types of chores they used to do when they were younger. Write a response to the magazine.

Paso 1 Jot down the chores that had to be done around the house while you were growing up. Next to each of the chores write the name of the person that used to do it.

Paso 2 Begin your paragraph by explaining who lived in your household when you were younger and whether you lived in a house or an apartment. Then, using the information you generated in **Paso 1,** indicate who used to do which chores around the house. Because you are describing what you and others used to do, you will need to use the imperfect.

© Denizo71/Shuttestock

Paso 3 Edit your paragraph:

    1. Do the verbs agree with the subject?

    2. Are there any spelling errors? Did you use accents on the imperfect forms that require them?

_____

_____

_____

_____

_____

_____

_____

Prueba tu vocabulario 2

8.17 **La palabra escondida** Use the clues to find the hidden word.

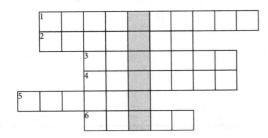

1. Las _____ es un juego en donde un niño busca a los otros niños.

2. Los niños deben pedirle _____ a sus padres para ir a casa de sus amigos.

3. A muchas niñas les gusta jugar con sus _____.

4. Por la noche, algunos padres les leen _____ a sus hijos, por ejemplo, el de "La Bella Durmiente".

5. Una actividad popular entre los niños de todo el mundo es _____ la cuerda.

6. Muchos niños aprenden a tocar el _____.

¿Cuál es la palabra escondida? _____

8.18 **Las actividades** Match the definition with the activity or game.

1. _____ Es un juego de mesa para dos personas.   **a.** el osito

2. _____ Es un animal de juguete.   **b.** la cometa

3. _____ Es una historia corta y cómica.   **c.** el chiste

4. _____ Es una actividad que les encanta a muchas abuelas. **d.** el ajedrez

5. _____ Es un juguete popular cuando hace viento.   **e.** tejer

6. _____ Requiere papel y lápices y un poco de talento artístico. **f.** dibujar

8.19 **¿Qué hacían?** Describe the activities that the people in the illustration used to do.

Modelo   José y su padre *jugaban con una pelota.*

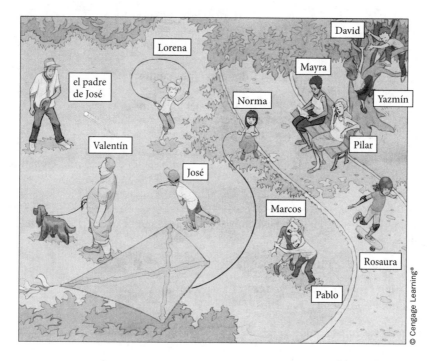

1. Rosaura _____.

2. Norma _____.

3. Marcos y Pablo _____.

4. Lorena _____.

5. David y Yazmín _____.

Prueba tu gramática 3 y 4

Indirect object pronouns

8.20 **Día de los Reyes** Jesús has five nephews and nieces, and he wants to give each one of them something on Three Kings Day. Complete each sentence with the appropriate indirect object pronoun.

1. _____ llevo el juego de damas a Lilian y a Marco.

2. _____ llevo la patineta a Lili.

3. _____ llevo el osito de peluche a Ana.

4. _____ llevo varios videojuegos a Gustavo y a Ricardito.

5. _____ llevo unas historietas a todos.

8.21 **Mis hijos** Dalia is talking about her twin children. Complete her sentences with the indirect object pronoun and the appropriate form of the verb in parentheses.

1. A mi hijo _____ _____ (encantar) trepar árboles.

2. A mi hija _____ _____ (aburrir) jugar en el jardín.

3. A ella _____ _____ (interesar) los cuentos.

4. A los dos _____ _____ (fascinar) los libros y

   _____ _____ (importar) aprender a leer bien.

5. A mi esposo y a mí _____ _____ (molestar) cuando nuestros hijos pelean.

8.22 **Reacciones** Decide which verb best completes each sentence and write complete sentences using the elements given.

   aburrir   caer mal   encantar   preocupar

   Modelo   el niño / los carritos – fascinar
   Al niño le fascinan los carritos.

1. la madre / la salud de sus hijos _____

2. la niñera / los niños que se portan mal _____

3. las niñas / jugar con muñecas _____

4. los niños / la tarea _____

8.23 **La ayuda** Lilia and Clara are helping their father to tidy up the house because they want to surprise their mother. Complete their dialogue with the missing indirect object pronouns.

CLARA: Papá, ¿(1.) _____ ayudo a limpiar?

PAPÁ: Sí, hija. Por favor ¿(2.) _____ puedes traer una escoba?

CLARA: Sí, papá, enseguida (3.) _____ traigo una escoba.

LILIA: Papá, yo (4.) _____ quiero ayudar también. Si quieres

(5.) _____ puedo guardar sus juguetes a mi hermanito.

PAPÁ: ¡Muy buena idea! (6.) _____ vamos a dar una gran sorpresa a mamá.

LILIA: ¡Sí! y ella (7.) _____ va a preparar un pastel para darnos las gracias.

PAPÁ: ¡Qué interesada!... pero tienes razón ¡sus pasteles son deliciosos!

8.24 **En el café** A couple is dining at a café with their three-year-old son, who is very curious about his surroundings. Complete their conversation with the correct indirect object pronouns.

CARLITOS: Mamá, ¿quién es ese hombre que (1.) _____ lleva sándwiches a aquella familia?

MAMÁ: Él es un mesero que trabaja aquí en el café.

CARLITOS: ¿Y por qué no (2.) _____ trae un sándwich a mí? Tengo hambre.

PAPÁ: El mesero pronto (3.) _____ va a traer el menú a tu mamá y a mí. Tenemos que leer el menú para saber qué tipo de sándwiches hay.

CARLITOS: Pues… quiero un sándwich de pollo.

MAMÁ: Seguramente aquí los venden. El mesero (4.) _____ puede servir uno con papas fritas.

CARLITOS: ¡Mira, papá! Esa señora olvidó el dinero en la mesa.

PAPÁ: Ay, no, hijo. Es que ella (5.) _____ dejó una propina al mesero.

CARLITOS: ¿Una propina? ¿Qué es eso?

MAMÁ: Es dinero que (6.) _____ damos a los meseros por trabajar tan duro *(hard)*.

CARLITOS: Mamá, estoy aburrido. Quiero jugar.

MAMÁ: (7.) _____ gusta dibujar, ¿verdad? Pues (8.) _____ podemos pedir al mesero unos lápices de color y un papel.

8.25 **Lo hacemos para otros** Using the elements given and the appropriate indirect object pronouns, write complete sentences telling what the following people do for others. Use the present tense.

1. la mamá / contar / cuentos / a los niños

_____

2. la niñera / dar / juegos de mesa / a Nayeli

_____

3. los niños / llevar / un osito / a su amigo enfermo

_____

4. los padres / comprar / videojuegos / a su hijo

_____

Double object pronouns

8.26 **De niño** Choose the appropriate answer for the following questions.

1. ¿Quién te compró tu primera bicicleta?

   a. Mis padres me la compraron.   **b.** Se la compré a mi hermano.

2. ¿Quién te leía cuentos?

   a. Mi madre me los leía.   **b.** Mi padre se los leía.

3. ¿A quién le dabas dibujos?

   a. Mi maestra me los daba.   **b.** Se los daba a mis abuelos.

4. ¿Quién te preparaba el almuerzo?

   a. Mi madre me lo preparaba.   **b.** Yo se lo preparaba.

5. ¿A quién le pedías permiso para salir?

   a. Mi hermano me lo pedía.   **b.** Se lo pedía a mi padre.

8.27 **Regalos de Navidad** Read the following conversation and complete it with the necessary direct and indirect object pronouns.

Félix: ¿Cómo pasaste la Navidad, Elena?

Elena: Muy bien. ¿Y tú?

Félix: Bien. Recibí una bicicleta.

Elena: ¡Qué padre! ¿Quién te (1.) _____ regaló?

Félix: Mis padres (2.) _____ (3.) _____ regalaron. ¿Qué (4.) _____ regalaron tus padres?

Elena: (5.) _____ dieron unos videojuegos.

Félix: ¡Qué bien! Oye, ¿me (6.) _____ prestas?

Elena: Por supuesto. (7.) _____ (8.) _____ presto si tú me prestas tu bicicleta.

Félix: Vale *(Okay)*, (9.) _____ (10.) _____ presto.

(MÁS TARDE)

Félix: Mamá, (11.) _____ voy a prestar mi bicicleta a Elena.

Mamá: ¿(12.) _____ (13.) _____ vas a prestar a Elena?

Félix: Sí, mamá. Y ella (14.) _____ va a prestar unos videojuegos.

Mamá: No quiero que (15.) _____ (16.) _____ prestes. Es nueva, hijo.

Félix: No pasa nada, mamá. Ella es muy responsable.

Mamá: Bueno, es tu bicicleta... pero si ella no te (17.) _____ devuelve, no (18.) _____ compro otra.

8.28 **¿Para quiénes son?** Gloria and Juan are taking their children on vacation. Gloria bought some items and the kids want to know who they are for. Answer the questions using both direct and indirect object pronouns. Follow the model.

Modelo   ¡Una guitarra! ¿Para quién es? (Mariana)
Se la compré a Mariana.

1. ¡Qué bonito traje de baño! ¿Para quién es? (para tu hermano)

_____

2. ¡Qué bellos patines! ¿Para quién son? (para tu papá)

_____

3. ¡Me gustan estas raquetas! ¿Para quién son? (para ti)

_____

4. ¡Qué lindo sombrero! ¿Para quién es? (para mí)

_____

5. ¡Una pelota grande! ¿Para quién es? (para tu hermano y para ti)

_____

6. ¡Unas toallas! ¿Para quién son? (para tu papá y para mí)

_____

8.29 **¿Me lo prestas?** Imagine that you are a child and a friend is always asking to borrow your things. Answer his questions using both direct and indirect object pronouns.

1. ¿Me prestas tus historietas? Sí, _____.

2. ¿Me prestas tus videojuegos? No, _____.

3. ¿Me prestas tu rompecabezas? No, _____.

4. ¿Me prestas tu guitarra? No, _____.

5. ¿Me prestas tus juegos de mesa? Sí, _____.

6. ¿Me prestas tu cometa? Sí, _____.

8.30 **Preguntas personales** Answer the questions in complete sentences, using both the direct and indirect object pronouns.

1. ¿A quién le compras regalos? _____

2. ¿Quién te da regalos a ti? _____

3. ¿A quién le escribes correos electrónicos? _____

4. ¿Quién te escribe correos electrónicos a ti? _____

5. ¿A quién le pides ayuda con tu tarea? _____

6. ¿Quién te pide ayuda a ti? _____

¡Hora de escuchar! 2

8.31 **¿A quién?** Ana Luisa babysat two young children yesterday. Listen to her comments and decide
3-5   if the following statements refer to Luli, Marcos or both children (**Los dos**).

1. Tiene una colección.   **a.** Luli   **b.** Marcos   **c.** Los dos

2. Le gusta dibujar.   **a.** Luli   **b.** Marcos   **c.** Los dos

3. Jugó al dominó.   **a.** Luli   **b.** Marcos   **c.** Los dos

4. Escuchó un cuento.   **a.** Luli   **b.** Marcos   **c.** Los dos

5. Saltó en la cama.   **a.** Luli   **b.** Marcos   **c.** Los dos

8.32 **¿Cierto o falso?** Listen to the the statements made by different people talking about how they
3-6   like to spend their free time. Then decide if the statements below are true (**cierto**) or false (**falso**).

1. Cierto   Falso   Le aburre estar en casa.

2. Cierto   Falso   Le gusta mucho escuchar música.

3. Cierto   Falso   Le cae muy bien su hermano.

4. Cierto   Falso   Le encanta jugar al dominó.

8.33 **Cuando vivía en Argentina** Listen to Camila's story about her childhood and answer the
3-7   questions.

1. ¿Adónde se fue a vivir la familia de Camila? _____

2. ¿Dónde estaba la escuela de Camila? _____

3. ¿A qué jugaba en el parque? _____

4. ¿Qué hacía con sus amigos cuando la visitaban en casa? _____

5. ¿Qué hacía la mamá de Camila? _____

¡Hora de reciclar! 2

8.34 **El pretérito** Complete the following story with the verbs in the preterite.

Ayer yo (1.) _____ (tener) que cuidar a mi sobrino porque mi hermana y su esposo

(2.) _____ (ir) de compras. Ellos (3.) _____ (llegar) a mi casa a las 4:00 de la tarde

y me (4.) _____ (prometer) regresar a las siete de la noche. Yo (5.) _____ (llevar)

a Fernandito al parque, pero él (6.) _____ (portarse) muy mal y (yo) (7.) _____

(decidir) regresar a casa. Yo (8.) _____ (poner) la televisión para entretener a Fernandito.

El teléfono (9.) _____ (sonar) y yo (10.) _____ (ir) a contestarlo. Cuando

(11.) _____ (regresar), Fernandito no estaba frente al televisor... yo ¡(12.) _____

(asustarse *to get scared*) mucho! Entonces yo (13.) _____ (correr) a la puerta... y allí estaba

Fernandito. ¡Él (14.) _____ (ir) a abrirles la puerta a sus papás! ¡Qué susto!

8.35 *Por y para* Complete the following paragraph by filling in the blanks with **por** or **para**.

(1.) _____ ser el cumpleaños de mi sobrino, tuve que comprarle un regalo. Llamé a mi hermana

ayer (2.) _____ la mañana (3.) _____ saber qué juguetes le gustan. Me recomendó

buscar un carrito (4.) _____ su colección. Fui a varias tiendas (5.) _____ buscar su

regalo y (6.) _____ fin encontré uno que me gustaba. Lo compré (7.) _____ 150 pesos

y salí (8.) _____ la casa de mi hermana (9.) _____ asistir a la fiesta de mi sobrino.

(10.) _____ supuesto, llegué tarde, pero a mi sobrino le gustó mucho el regalo.

CAPÍTULO 9   ¿Qué pasó?

Prueba tu vocabulario 1

9.1 **La boda** Complete the paragraph with the logical vocabulary word.

Ayer fue la boda de Sara y Manuel y fue muy bonita. Nosotros recibimos la (1.) _____ hace

un mes *(one month ago)* y les compramos un (2.) _____ en una tienda de artículos para la casa.

El día de la boda había muchos (3.) _____ en la iglesia. Después de la misa, fuimos al

salón de fiestas, en donde un (4.) _____ tocaba música para bailar. Para comer, ofrecieron

varios tipos de (5.) _____. Brindamos con (6.) _____. Al final de la

fiesta los novios cortaron el (7.) _____, que era de chocolate.

_____

9.2 **Definiciones** Read each definition and write the vocabulary word to which it refers. Be sure to include the definite article.

1. _____ Las ponemos en un pastel; el número que ponemos es igual al número de

años que cumple la persona.

2. _____ Es muy popular en las fiestas de niños. Se llena con dulces y se rompe.

3. _____ Es una celebración donde dos personas aceptan ser esposo y esposa.

4. _____ Es un evento en donde muchas personas caminan por la calle con trajes de

colores y tocan música mientras la gente los ve.

5. _____ Son de colores y se usan para celebrar el Día de la Independencia y otros días

festivos. Los vemos en el cielo *(sky)*.

6. _____ En una fiesta de cumpleaños, la persona que cumple años los abre después de

cortar el pastel.

_____

9.3 **La lógica** Circle the word that does not belong in each list.

1. el pastel, los bocadillos, los dulces, el champán

2. el bautizo, los quinceaños, el desfile, el santo

3. la invitación, el grupo de música, los globos, las decoraciones

4. los novios, los fuegos artificiales, el brindis, el pastel

Prueba tu gramática 1 y 2

A comparison of the preterite and imperfect

9.4 **La Navidad** Complete the following sentences with the necessary conjugation of the verbs in parentheses. Pay attention to the uses of preterite and imperfect.

La escena

(1.) _____ (Ser) Navidad y (2.) _____ (hacer) frío afuera. Dentro de la casa,

nadie (3.) _____ (tener) frío porque todos (4.) _____ (dormir) en sus camas.

En la sala, (5.) _____ (haber) un árbol de Navidad con regalos para todos.

La acción

A las siete de la mañana, los niños (6.) _____ (despertarse) y (7.) _____

(ir) al cuarto de sus padres para despertarlos. Una vez que ellos (8.) _____ (levantarse),

los niños (9.) _____ (correr) a la sala para abrir sus regalos. Poco después sus padres

(10.) _____ (llegar) cansados, pero con una sonrisa (*smile*).

9.5 **¿Qué pasaba?** Look at the image. Using the imperfect, describe what was happening when the photographer took this picture.

Cuando el fotógrafo sacó esta foto…

1. los novios _____ .

2. Javier _____ .

3. Marcia y Pati _____ .

4. Alex _____ .

5. el grupo musical _____ .

9.6 **¿Qué pasó?** The initial part of this story sets the scene and uses the imperfect. Complete the remainder of the narration using the preterite of the verbs in parentheses.

Era el Día de los Muertos y yo estaba sentada en el cementerio. Había flores y velas por todas partes. Todo

estaba muy tranquilo cuando de repente *(suddenly)* yo (1.) _____ (escuchar) un ruido *(noise)*.

(2.) _____ (Mirar) a mi izquierda y (3.) _____ (ver) una silueta.

(4.) _____ (Asustarse *to get scared*) y (5.) _____ (decidir) volver a mi casa.

(6.) _____ (Levantarse) y (7.) _____ (empezar) a caminar hacia la puerta. Luego

(8.) _____ (oír) mi nombre y (9.) _____ (reconocer) la voz *(voice)* de mi hermano.

Él también (10.) _____ (traer) flores para la abuela.

9.7 **Mis cumpleaños** Write three sentences in which you describe what you used to do on your birthday when you were a child. Then write three more sentences in which you tell what you did on your last birthday.

1. Cuando era niño(a)…

   a. _____

   b. _____

   c. _____

2. El día de mi último cumpleaños…

   a. _____

   b. _____

   c. _____

Uses of the preterite and imperfect

9.8 **La fiesta** Using the words in parentheses, tell what Julio <u>was doing</u> while Marta was preparing for the party. **¡OJO!** These actions are both going on at the same time, so remember to use the imperfect.

Modelo (comprar estampillas [stamps])
Mientras Marta escribía las invitaciones, Julio *compraba estampillas*.

1. (limpiar la casa)

   Mientras Marta compraba la comida, Julio _____.

2. (seleccionar el vino)

   Mientras Marta preparaba la comida, Julio _____.

3. (poner la mesa)

   Mientras Marta lavaba los platos, Julio _____.

4. (afeitarse)

   Mientras Marta se vestía, Julio _____.

5. (servir las bebidas)

   Mientras Marta les abría la puerta a los invitados, Julio _____.

6. (divertirse)

   Mientras Marta trabajaba en la cocina, Julio y los invitados _____.

9.9 **Después** Using logic, decide which of the two activities happened first. Then write a sentence telling what the bride and groom did. **¡OJO!** These actions are sequenced, so remember to use the preterite.

Modelo decidir casarse / enamorarse
Los novios se enamoraron y después decidieron casarse.

1. poner una fecha / mandar las invitaciones

   _____

2. escoger (*to choose*) el menú / encontrar un salón de fiestas

   _____

3. ir a la recepción / casarse en la iglesia

   _____

4. cortar el pastel / servir el pastel

   _____

5. tomar champán / hacer un brindis

   _____

9.10 **El día de la fiesta** Complete the sentences in a logical manner. Pay attention to the uses of the preterite and the imperfect.

1. Después de que Lore les mandó invitaciones a sus amigos, _____.

2. Mientras la mamá de Lore estaba en la cocina, _____.

3. Mientras sus amigos bailaban, Lore _____.

4. Cuando Lore apagó las velas de su pastel, _____.

5. Cuando la fiesta terminó, los invitados _____.

¡Hora de escuchar! 1

9.11 **La respuesta** Listen to the questions carefully and circle the best response.
3-8

1. **a.** Debes mandar regalos.   **b.** Debes mandar invitaciones.

2. **a.** champán y bocadillos   **b.** globos y banderines

3. **a.** un grupo musical y una serenata   **b.** las posadas

4. **a.** regalos   **b.** desfiles

9.12 **¿Descripción o narración?** Listen to the paragraphs and decide whether the person is
3-9   describing the scene (**descripción**) or narrating the events or actions of a story (**narración**).

1. descripción   narración

2. descripción   narración

3. descripción   narración

4. descripción   narración

5. descripción   narración

🔊 **9.13** **El gruñón** Listen as Édgar tells about a party he attended, and decide if the statements below are
3-10   true (**cierto**) or false (**falso**).

1. Cierto Falso La fiesta era para celebrar el cumpleaños de Édgar.

2. Cierto Falso Todos se divertían cuando alguien llamó por teléfono.

3. Cierto Falso Un policía llamó por teléfono.

4. Cierto Falso Los policías vinieron a la fiesta porque hacían mucho ruido.

¡Hora de reciclar! 1

9.14 **Los pronombres de objeto indirecto** Using indirect object pronouns and the present tense
of the verbs in parentheses, state what each person does for another person. Follow the model.

   Modelo   Pepe quiere una piñata.   Su madre *le compra* (comprar) una piñata.

1. Queremos comer postre. El mesero _____ (traer) pastel.

2. Adrián quiere casarse (*to marry*) con Rebeca. Él _____ (pedir) matrimonio.

3. Hoy es tu cumpleaños. Yo _____ (dar) un regalo.

4. Yo voy a hacer un brindis. El mesero _____ (servir) champán.

5. Ustedes van a tener una recepción después de la boda. El chef _____ (preparar) una gran comida.

9.15 **El imperfecto** Maite is reminiscing about the parties of her youth. Complete her description with
the correct imperfect form of the appropriate verb from the list.

comer	comprar	correr	dar	estar
gustar	jugar	preparar	romper	ser

Cuando yo (1.) _____ niña, mis padres siempre nos (2.) _____ fiestas en nuestros

cumpleaños. Mi madre (3.) _____ todas las comidas que más nos (4.) _____ a mis

hermanos y a mí. Recuerdo muy bien las piñatas que ella (5.) _____ en el supermercado. Cuando

uno de nosotros (6.) _____ la piñata todos los niños (7.) _____ para recoger los

dulces. Después (8.) _____ el pastel y luego (9.) _____ en el jardín. ¡Siempre (10.)

_____ muy contentos!

¡Hora de escribir!

Write a two-paragraph essay about a favorite childhood holiday.

Paso 1 Think of the holiday you enjoyed most when you were younger; was it Thanksgiving (**Día de Acción de Gracias**), Hannukah, Halloween, Christmas (**Navidad**), Easter (**Pascua**), or another holiday? Write down a list of phrases that describe what the weather was normally like during that day and also what you and your family would usually do to celebrate.

© Monkey Business Images/Shutterstock

Paso 2 Now think about one year where something unusual or memorable happened during your favorite holiday. Jot down phrases that set the scene of this particular day, such as your age, the weather, and what you and your family were doing.

Paso 3 Write a list of phrases to tell what happened that day that was so unusual or memorable.

Paso 4 Write your first paragraph, using the information you generated in **Paso 1.** Use the imperfect tense in your descriptions.

Paso 5 Using the information you generated in **Paso 2,** begin your second paragraph with a sentence or two that sets the scene (imperfect). Then use the information you generated in **Paso 3** to complete your paragraph, telling what happened that particular day (preterite).

Paso 6 Edit your paragraphs:

    1. Do you have smooth transitions between sentences? Between the two paragraphs?
    2. Do verbs agree with the subject?
    3. Thinking about what you learned in this lesson, have you used the preterite and the imperfect appropriately?
    4. Are there any spelling errors? Do the verbs that need accents have them?

_____

_____

_____

_____

_____

_____

_____

_____

_____

_____

Prueba tu vocabulario 2

9.16 **¿Qué hay?** Label the vocabulary in the drawing.

1. _____
2. _____
3. _____
4. _____
5. _____
6. _____

© Cengage Learning®

9.17 **¿Qué es?** Read the definitions and write the vocabulary words to which they refer.

1. _____ Es el automóvil que conduce un policía.

2. _____ Es un verbo para describir un accidente en el que un auto choca con una persona.

3. _____ Tiene tres luces que controlan el tráfico.

4. _____ Es un verbo que significa que una persona pierde la concentración.

5. _____ Es una persona que conduce su auto por la calle.

6. _____ Es la persona que ve un accidente.

9.18 **En la calle** Complete the statements with a logical word from the list.

accidente	ambulancia	avenida	camilla	cruce
límite de velocidad	multa	paramédico	peatón	señal

1. Usamos la _____ para llevar a los heridos a la ambulancia.

2. Un semáforo es un tipo de _____ de tránsito.

3. El accidente ocurrió porque el conductor no paró en el _____.

4. Cuando camino por la calle no soy un conductor, soy un _____.

5. Hay que respetar el _____ para no recibir multas por ir muy rápido.

Prueba tu gramática 3 y 4

Preterite and imperfect with emotions and mental states

9.19 **¿Cómo se sintieron?** Choose the most appropriate verb to complete the ideas. You will have to decide if you need preterite or imperfect.

aburrirse	alegrarse	asustarse	enojarse	frustrarse	sorprenderse

1. Cuando mis amigos me dieron una fiesta sorpresa, (yo) _____.

2. Cuando mi novia me propuso matrimonio, (yo) _____.

3. De niña, mi hermana era muy miedosa y _____ cuando había tormentas (storms).

4. Ayer nadie hizo la tarea y el profesor _____.

5. Antes (yo) _____ cuando no entendía todo lo que decía el profesor.

6. De niño, José _____ en sus clases de matemáticas porque no le interesaban.

9.20 **Oraciones incompletas** Complete the following sentences. **¡OJO!** You will need to pay attention to whether the verb is in the preterite or the imperfect.

1. Esta mañana había _____.

2. Una vez me enojé cuando _____.

3. Nunca pude _____.

4. Cuando era niño(a), siempre quería _____.

5. Conocí a _____.

9.21 **Un accidente** Conjugate the verbs in the appropriate form of the preterite or imperfect as necessary.

1. Ayer _____ (haber) un accidente en la calle Serrano.

2. Cuando salí de mi casa no _____ (saber) del accidente.

3. Llegué a la intersección y vi que nadie _____ (poder) atravesar.

4. Yo no _____ (querer) llegar tarde para mi primera clase porque teníamos un examen.

5. (Yo) _____ (tener) que buscar otra ruta y al final _____ (poder) llegar

   a tiempo.

9.22 **Un accidente poco común** Complete the following paragraph with the correct preterite or imperfect form of the verb in parentheses.

El otro día mis padres y yo (1.) _____ (estar) en la sala. (Nosotros) (2.) _____

(mirar) la tele y (3.) _____ (tomar) refrescos. De repente, (4.) _____ (haber)

un ruido terrible. (Yo) no (5.) _____ (saber) lo que (6.) _____ (pasar) y

(7.) _____ (correr) a la ventana. ¡No (8.) _____ (poder) creerlo! Mi abuela

(9.) _____ (venir) a visitarnos y, al llegar, (10.) _____ (chocar) con el coche de mi

papá. Mi papá (11.) _____ (asustarse) y (12.) _____ (salir) corriendo de la casa para

ver a mi abuela. Cuando él (13.) _____ (saber) que ella no (14.) _____ (estar) herida,

(15.) _____ (enojarse) con ella por chocar con su coche. Mi abuela (16.) _____

(empezar) a reírse porque ella (17.) _____ (estar) muy nerviosa. ¡Qué susto!

Preterite and imperfect: A summary

9.23 **¿Qué ocurrió?** The police department received several reports of accidents. Help them complete the reports with the most logical verb tense (preterite or imperfect) of the verbs in parentheses.

1. Un peatón (a.) _____ (cruzar) la calle mientras (b.) _____ (leer) el periódico.

   Un ciclista (c.) _____ (ir) muy rápido por la calle y (d.) _____ (atropellar) al

   peatón. El peatón (e.) _____ (estar) inconsciente cuando la ambulancia (f.) _____

   (llegar). El ciclista (g.) _____ (romperse) una pierna.

2. Un automovilista (a.) _____ (hablar) por teléfono mientras (b.) _____ (conducir)

   y no (c.) _____ (prestar) atención. De repente (d.) _____ (ver) a un gato que

   (e.) _____ (cruzar) la calle. El automovilista (f.) _____ (asustarse) y

   (g.) _____ (chocar) con un coche estacionado en la calle.

9.24 **Explicaciones** Look at Activity 9.23. Then decide which of the following reasons explains why you chose the verb form you did.

A. an action in progress in the past

B. a description of a condition in the past

C. a completed action in the past

D. a change of emotion or mental state

1. a. _____   **2.** a. _____

b. _____   b. _____

c. _____   c. _____

d. _____   d. _____

e. _____   e. _____

f. _____   f. _____

g. _____   g. _____

9.25 **Un suceso fuera de este mundo** Look at the drawing and tell the story of what happened. Use the preterite and imperfect, as well as the verbs provided and others you have learned in this chapter. Be sure to give plenty of details and a conclusion to the story.

Vocabulario útil: **ir de compras** *to go shopping* **robar** *to rob* **pegar** *to hit*

© Cengage Learning®

_____

_____

_____

_____

_____

¡Hora de escuchar! 2

🔊 **9.26** **¿Es lógico?** You will hear five statements. Decide whether they are logical (**lógico**) or illogical (**ilógico**).
3-11

1. lógico   ilógico

2. lógico   ilógico

3. lógico   ilógico

4. lógico   ilógico

5. lógico   ilógico

🔊 **9.27** **¿Pretérito o imperfecto?** You will hear five different situations. Choose the appropriate explanation for each one.
3-12

1. **a.** Nos conocíamos en la universidad.   **b.** Nos conocimos en la universidad.

2. **a.** Había muchos accidentes.   **b.** Hubo muchos accidentes.

3. **a.** No sabía conducir.   **b.** No supe conducir.

4. **a.** No podía ver las señales.   **b.** No pude ver las señales.

5. **a.** No quería prestarme su coche.   **b.** No quiso prestarme su coche.

🔊 **9.28** **¿Cierto o falso?** Listen as Sofía describes an accident she had. Decide whether the following statements are true (**cierto**) or false (**falso**).
3-13

1. Cierto   Falso   Sofía fue a correr con su perro el sábado.

2. Cierto   Falso   Había un gato en un coche.

3. Cierto   Falso   El automovilista atropelló al perro.

4. Cierto   Falso   Sofía tuvo que pagar por los daños al coche.

¡Hora de reciclar! 2

9.29 **Las expresiones negativas** You had an accident and your friend wants to know more about what happened. Answer his questions in complete sentences using the negative expressions you learned in the last chapter.

1. No me gusta conducir por la calle Santos, ¿y a ti? _____

2. ¿Había algo en la calle? _____

3. ¿Llamaron a la policía o a los paramédicos? _____

4. ¿Alguien está herido? _____

9.30 **Los pronombres de objeto directo e indirecto** It is December 25 and everyone has opened their gifts. Answer these questions, using both direct and indirect object pronouns and the information in parentheses.

1. ¿Quién le regaló el juego de mesa a Lucía? (su madre)

_____

2. ¿Quién nos regaló la cometa a Héctor y a mí? (la señora Conde)

_____

3. ¿Quiénes les regalaron las muñecas a las niñas? (sus padres)

_____

4. ¿Quién les regaló el piano a Jaime y a Carmen? (su abuela)

_____

5. ¿Quién te regaló los carritos? (Octavio)

_____

6. ¿Quiénes me regalaron los videojuegos? (tus padres)

_____

CAPÍTULO 10 ¿Adónde vas a viajar?

Prueba tu vocabulario 1

10.1 **Palabras escondidas** Unscramble the vocabulary words.

1. doomrtasr _____: Lugar donde facturamos las maletas

2. tnoeisa _____: Lugar en el que nos sentamos en el avión

3. laqualti _____: Lugar donde se pueden comprar los boletos de tren

4. jueqaipe _____: Todas las maletas que se llevan al viajar

5. rapada _____: Cuando se hace un alto en un viaje por autobús

6. asorjpea _____: Persona que viaja en un tren o avión

7. astoppare _____: Un documento necesario para salir del país

---

10.2 **Conclusiones** Complete each of the following ideas by matching it to a logical conclusion in the second column.

1. _____ Estoy esperando desde las 11:00 y el avión todavía no llega.   **a.** Pido la ventanilla.

2. _____ Falta media hora para la salida de mi vuelo.   **b.** Está retrasado.

3. _____ Me gusta ver el paisaje *(landscape)* cuando viajo.   **c.** Me voy a poner el cinturón de seguridad.

4. _____ ¡El avión ya va a despegar!   **d.** Por eso llevo solo equipaje de mano.

5. _____ Tengo poco tiempo para tomar mi conexión.   **e.** Voy a esperar en la sala de espera.

10.3 **¿En dónde?** Complete the sentences with the most logical place from the list below.

la aduana	el pasillo	la primera clase	el mostrador
la puerta de salida	el reclamo de equipaje	la revisión de equipaje	la sala de espera

1. Para abordar el avión salgo por _____.

2. Espero para recoger todas mis maletas en _____.

3. Camino por _____ para estirarme un poco durante el vuelo.

4. Recibo mi pase de abordar en _____.

5. Me traen comida buena y bebidas gratis *(free)* a mi asiento, y hay una asistente de vuelo

   para 12 pasajeros en _____.

10.4 **Definiciones** Write a definition in Spanish for each of the vocabulary words below.

1. la ventanilla _____

2. la primera clase _____

3. la visa _____

4. el andén _____

5. el revisor _____

6. la sala de espera _____

7. la escala _____

8. el pase de abordar _____

Prueba tu gramática 1 y 2

Relative pronouns and adverbs

10.5 *Que, quien* o *quienes* Select the relative pronoun that completes the statement correctly.

1. Los pasajeros (que / quienes) viajaban desde Paraguay estaban muy cansados por el largo viaje.

2. El autobús (que / quien) está en la parada sale en cinco minutos.

3. Ahora no veo al agente con (que / quien) hablé.

4. No encuentro las maletas (que / quienes) facturé al salir.

5. Mis amigos están en el avión (que / quien) aterriza ahora.

6. Muchos de los pasajeros con (que / quienes) viajé eran muy impacientes.

10.6 **Conexiones** Complete the sentences with the appropriate pronoun: **que, quien, quienes,** or **donde.**

1. Hay alguien en mi familia _____ viaja mucho.

2. La taquilla _____ compré el boleto está cerrada ahora.

3. Algunos pasajeros, _____ todavía están en la aduana, van a perder el vuelo.

4. Tienes que mostrarle tu boleto al revisor _____ entró en el vagón.

5. Conozco a alguien _____ tiene miedo de viajar en avión.

6. Hay algunos turistas a _____ no les gusta viajar por tren.

10.7 **Oraciones sofisticadas** Create more sophisticated sentences by combining the two shorter sentences into one and using the pronouns **donde, que,** and **quien(es).**

1. Hay muchas personas. Estas personas prefieren viajar en tren.

_____

2. El revisor está en el tren. Yo le di mi boleto al revisor.

_____

3. Los pasajeros necesitan un pasaporte. Ellos viajan a otro país.

_____

4. Debes ir al andén número 6. El tren para Valencia está en el andén.

_____

5. Las personas esperan en el área de reclamo de equipaje. Ellas facturaron sus maletas en Miami.

_____

Formal and *nosotros* commands

10.8 **El asistente de vuelo** Complete the directions that the flight attendant gives to passengers, using formal **(ustedes)** commands and the verbs in parentheses.

1. Por favor, _____ (poner) su equipaje debajo de sus asientos.

2. No _____ (fumar) y _____ (escuchar) con atención la información de seguridad que les voy a dar.

3. Por favor, _____ (pagar) sus bebidas alcohólicas con tarjeta de crédito.

4. No _____ (caminar) por el pasillo cuando la señal del cinturón de seguridad esté encendida.

5. No _____ (usar) sus teléfonos celulares ni sus computadoras portátiles.

6. _____ (Mantener) el cinturón abrochado cuando estén sentados.

10.9 **Un viaje internacional** You are a travel agent giving tips to senior citizens who are traveling internationally for the first time. Choose the most logical ending for each piece of advice, and then write the full sentence using formal (**usted**) commands and the verbs indicated.

Modelo (llevar) Señorita Méndez   revistas para leer en el avión
Señorita Méndez, lleve revistas para leer en el avión.

1. _____ Señor Beltrán, (llegar)   **a.** sus maletas en el mostrador

2. _____ Señora Gómez, (no tener)   **b.** su pasaporte al personal de seguridad

3. _____ Señora del Valle, (mostrar)   **c.** dos horas antes de su vuelo

4. _____ Señor Morales, (facturar)   **d.** su equipaje en el reclamo de equipaje

5. _____ Señora Ortega, (buscar)   **e.** ningún líquido de más de tres onzas en su equipaje de mano

1. _____

2. _____

3. _____

4. _____

5. _____

10.10 **En el vuelo** Read the questions a passenger asks a flight attendant and write the flight attendant's answers, using formal commands.

Modelo ¿Podemos hablar con el piloto durante el vuelo?
No, *no hablen con el piloto durante el vuelo.*

1. ¿Podemos fumar en este vuelo?

No, _____.

2. ¿Podemos poner nuestras maletas debajo del asiento?

Sí, _____.

3. ¿Podemos usar nuestros teléfonos celulares ahora?

No, _____.

4. ¿Podemos caminar por el pasillo?

No, _____.

5. ¿Podemos jugar en nuestras computadoras ahora?

Sí, _____.

10.11 ¿Qué dicen? A group of office workers just won some money in the lottery. They are brainstorming how to use the money. Complete their ideas using **nosotros** commands and the verbs from the list.

comprar   conseguir   donar   hacer   ir   pintar

JOSEFINA: ¡(1.) _____ una nueva cafetera para la oficina!

RAMÓN: ¡(2.) _____ todos de viaje a la playa por un día!

LIDIA: ¡(3.) _____ la oficina de color rosado!

SELENA: ¡(4.) _____ el dinero a una organización de caridad!

ALFONSO: ¡(5.) _____ una fiesta sorpresa para nuestro jefe!

IGNACIO: ¿Están locos? Mejor (6.) _____ otro billete de lotería, para ver si ganamos más dinero.

¡Hora de escuchar! 1

10.12 De viaje You will hear several questions. Select the best answer for each one.
3-14

1. **a.** No, prefiero esperar aquí.   **b.** No, deseo sentarme cerca del pasillo.

2. **a.** Sí, tengo una maleta.   **b.** Sí, quiero comprar uno, gracias.

3. **a.** De la sala de espera.   **b.** De la puerta número 21.

4. **a.** Sí, aterriza en Madrid.   **b.** Sí, necesita darme su pase de abordar.

5. **a.** Sí, está atrasado.   **b.** Sí, ya aterrizó.

10.13 ¿Qué hacemos? Several passengers have issues and they speak with the airline staff. Listen to
3-15   their problems and choose the most logical answer.

1. **a.** Pongamos sus nombres en la lista de espera para el vuelo a las 5:00.

   b. Miremos los vuelos para Montevideo para mañana.

2. **a.** Saquen sus pases de abordar por favor.

   b. Busquen sus asientos.

3. **a.** Tome su equipaje por favor.

   b. Describa su maleta por favor.

4. **a.** Aborde el avión por favor.

   b. Vaya a hablar con el agente de seguridad.

🔊 **10.14** **En la estación** You will hear an announcement at the train station. Listen carefully and then
3-16   decide which of the two phrases best completes each statement.

1. El tren a Mendoza....
     a. va a llegar pronto.
     b. va a salir pronto.

2. El tren a Mendoza...
     a. sale del andén número ocho.
     b. sale del andén número dieciocho.

3. Los pasajeros deben...
     a. tener su boleto en la mano.
     b. comprar sus boletos en la taquilla.

4. El tren a Rosario...
     a. va a llegar a tiempo.
     b. va a llegar tarde.

5. Se les recomienda a los pasajeros...
     a. no llevar equipaje de mano.
     b. no aceptar objetos de personas que no conocen.

¡Hora de reciclar! 1

10.15 **El pretérito y el imperfecto 1** Complete the paragraph with the preterite or the imperfect of
the verbs in parentheses.

El verano pasado yo (1.) _____ (salir) de viaje porque (2.) _____ (querer)

viajar por toda España. El primer día del viaje (3.) _____ (llegar) al aeropuerto muy

temprano, pero el vuelo (4.) _____ (estar) retrasado. Yo (5.) _____ (esperar)

por tres horas y media. Finalmente, todos los pasajeros y yo (6.) _____ (abordar) el avión.

(7.) _____ (Ser) las siete de la mañana cuando (nosotros) (8.) _____

(aterrizar) en Barcelona. Inmediatamente un autobús me (9.) _____ (llevar) a mi hostal que

(10.) _____ (ser) muy simple, pero muy barato. Así (11.) _____ (empezar) el

mejor viaje de mi vida. En total yo (12.) _____ (estar) en España por veintitrés días.

10.16 **Las expresiones negativas** Read the statements below, and change them to the negative.

> **Modelo** Siempre viajo en avión.
> *Nunca viajo en avión.*

1. Tengo <u>algunas</u> maletas para facturar.

   _____

2. Los asistentes de vuelo le ofrecieron bebidas a <u>todos</u>.

   _____

3. Compramos <u>algo</u> de comer en la sala de espera.

   _____

4. Para viajar yo necesitaba visa <u>y</u> pasaporte.

   _____

¡Hora de escribir!

Write the information for a webpage for tourists traveling to your region.

Paso 1 Jot down a list of recommendations you might give to someone traveling to your region for the first time. Think about what he or she might need to pack as well as information regarding arrival.

Paso 2 Think about the different attractions that your community or region has to offer. Make a list of three "must-see" points of interest that you think would most appeal to international tourists and jot down some things they might do there.

© Coral Coolahan/Shutterstock

Paso 3 Write your first paragraph using the items you wrote down in **Paso 1**. Be sure to use formal commands when you give your advice.

Paso 4 Look at the information you wrote down in **Paso 2** and write a second paragraph in which you tell tourists the places they should visit in your region. Use formal commands to tell them what they should see or do there.

Paso 5 Edit your paragraphs:

1. Do you have smooth transitions between sentences? Between the two paragraphs?
2. Do adjectives agree with the object they describe?
3. Have you used the proper forms for any commands?

   _____

   _____

   _____

   _____

Prueba tu vocabulario 2

10.17 Sopa de letras Unscramble the letters to form vocabulary words.

1. aserlecas _____: Las puedes bajar desde el segundo piso para llegar al primer piso.

2. velal _____: La necesitas para abrir la puerta.

3. sheépud _____: Es una persona que se queda en un hotel.

4. lenalisc _____: Una habitación _____ tiene solo una cama.

5. sobnote _____: Él te ayuda a cargar las maletas.

6. nieecpórc _____: Te registras aquí.

10.18 No pertenece Circle the word that does not belong in each group.

1. el gerente, el camarero, el huésped, el botones

2. la recepción, el sauna, la piscina, el gimnasio

3. doble, sencilla, llave, triple

4. la habitación, la recepción, el ascensor, el alojamiento

10.19 En el hotel Complete the statements with the logical conclusion from the second column.

1. _____ El ascensor no funciona...

2. _____ Debo imprimir unos documentos para mi conferencia...

3. _____ No estoy contento con los servicios del hotel...

4. _____ Puedo leer mi correo electrónico desde la habitación...

5. _____ Al final de mis vacaciones en el hotel...

6. _____ No quiero bajar al restaurante...

a. puedo usar el Internet para pagar rápidamente y marcharme.

b. así que voy a hablar con el gerente.

c. por eso subo por las escaleras.

d. y por eso pido servicio a la habitación.

e. así que voy al centro de negocios del hotel.

f. porque hay Internet inalámbrico.

10.20 ¿Es lógico? Read the following sentences and decide if they are logical or illogical.

1. lógico   ilógico   El hotel es de lujo y no tiene ni Internet inalámbrico ni sala de conferencias.

2. lógico   ilógico   Pido una habitación triple porque voy con dos amigos.

3. lógico   ilógico   La camarera nos dio la llave en la recepción.

4. lógico   ilógico   Nos vamos a quedar tres noches en este hotel porque hay habitaciones disponibles.

5. lógico   ilógico   El botones subió las maletas a la habitación.

Prueba tu gramática 3 y 4

Informal commands

10.21 Un viaje Your son is going to travel with some friends for the weekend and stay in a hotel. Complete the following recommendations for him with the appropriate form of the informal command (**tú**) of the verb in parentheses.

1. _____ (Hacer) una reservación antes de viajar.

2. _____ (Poner) tu traje de baño en la maleta para poder ir a la piscina.

3. _____ (Ir) a la recepción si tienes problemas.

4. _____ (Pagar) con tu tarjeta de crédito.

5. No _____ (dejar) nada valioso en la habitación.

6. No _____ (perder) la llave.

7. No _____ (pedir) servicio a la habitación porque cuesta mucho.

8. No _____ (hacer) llamadas telefónicas de tu habitación.

10.22 Los huéspedes A family is staying at a hotel, and they have many recommendations for their daughter. Complete them with the informal commands (**tú**) of the verbs in parentheses.

MAMÁ: Hija, ¡hace buen tiempo! (1.) _____ (Buscar) tu traje de baño y

(2.) _____ (ir) a la piscina para nadar.

PAPÁ: Pero no (3.) _____ (hablar) con personas que no conoces. (4.) _____

(Tomar) un poco de dinero de mi cartera por si necesitas comprar algo.

MAMÁ: Vamos a comer a las 3:00, así que (5.) _____ (volver) a la habitación a las 2:30, y así te

puedes cambiar de ropa antes de ir al restaurante.

PAPÁ: (6.) _____ (Recordar) que vamos a ir de paseo al centro por la tarde, entonces no

(7.) _____ (hacer) otros planes.

HIJA: Está bien, nos vemos a las 2:30, pero mamá, por favor no (8.) _____ (ir) a buscarme a

la piscina.

10.23 **Algunos consejos** Read the letter and write the informal commands (**tú**) of the verbs in parentheses.

Querido amigo:

Sé que vas a vivir un año con una familia en México y quiero darte unos consejos para que disfrutes

(you enjoy) más de tu tiempo en México. En primer lugar, la hora de la comida es muy importante.

(1.) _____ (Llegar) a tiempo y no (2.) _____ (pensar) que vas a comer frente al

televisor. Es la hora de hablar y convivir. Después de comer, (3.) _____ (ayudar) a recoger la

mesa y a lavar los platos. No todas las familias tienen lavaplatos, y muchos piensan que estas máquinas

desperdician *(waste)* agua.

En segundo lugar, ¡no (4.) _____ (usar) el teléfono mucho! Lo debes usar solo en caso de

una emergencia o para llamadas muy cortas. Si quieres hablar con tus amigos, (5.) _____

(hacer) una cita para verlos en un café. En varios países de Latinoamérica tienen que pagar por cada

minuto de uso del teléfono.

En tercer lugar, (6.) _____ (limpiar) tu dormitorio y no (7.) _____ (invitar) a

tus amigos del sexo opuesto a entrar en tu dormitorio… ¡algunas familias son muy tradicionales!

Finalmente, algo muy simple: no (8.) _____ (subir) los pies a los muebles nunca… ese fue

mi primer error.

Mi consejo más importante es: siempre (9.) _____ (ser) amable. Por ejemplo,

(10.) _____ (pedir) las cosas diciendo "por favor" y siempre (11.) _____ (dar)

las gracias. ¡(12.) _____ (Seguir) mis consejos y tu estancia con una familia mexicana será

inolvidable!

¡Buena suerte!

10.24 **Tus recomendaciones** Write four recommendations for someone coming from Latin America to study in the United States. Use two affirmative **tú** commands and two negative **tú** commands.

1. _____

2. _____

3. _____

4. _____

Commands with pronouns

10.25 **La manera correcta** A manager at the hotel is giving some advice to two new maids. Complete her statements with the affirmative command form of the verb used in the first part of the sentence. Be sure to use the direct object pronoun, as in the model. Use the same verb from the first command unless another verb is given.

Modelo No hagan la cama primero; *háganla* después de limpiar el baño.

1. No pongan toallas nuevas todos los días; _____ solamente si los huéspedes las piden.

2. No pasen la aspiradora antes de sacudir; _____ al final.

3. No abran la puerta de inmediato; _____ después de llamar para saber si hay alguien.

4. No dejen los platos sucios del servicio a la habitación; _____ (llevarse) con ustedes.

5. No limpien los baños con la aspiradora; _____ con un trapeador.

6. No muevan las pertenencias *(belongings)* de los huéspedes y tampoco _____ (tocar).

10.26 **Hora de dormir** You are staying in a hotel with your six-year old nephew. It is time for him to go to bed. For each of the requests he makes, use informal commands (**tú**) and the appropriate pronouns to tell him to do the opposite of what he wants to do.

Modelo Quiero comer mis chocolates. *No los comas.*
No quiero tomar la leche. *Tómala.*

1. Quiero ver este programa ahora. _____

2. No quiero bañarme. _____

3. No quiero ponerme la pijama. _____

4. Quiero leer un cuento. _____

5. Quiero escuchar mi música. _____

6. No quiero acostarme. _____

10.27 **La agencia de turismo** You have called an agency to help you plan a vacation. Answer their questions with formal commands, using the appropriate pronouns.

Modelo ¿Debo hacerles una reservación? *Sí, háganosla.*

1. ¿Debo buscarles un hotel? Sí, _____.

2. ¿Debo conseguirles un hotel con piscina? No, _____.

3. ¿Les recomiendo mi hotel favorito? No, _____.

4. ¿Les consigo un automóvil para alquilar? Sí, _____.

5. ¿Debo reservarles una habitación triple? No, _____.

¡Hora de escuchar! 2

🔊 10.28 ¿Quién es? Listen as each person tells what he or she is doing, then write in the blank who is
3-17 speaking.

botones   camarero   gerente   huésped   recepcionista

1. _____

2. _____

3. _____

4. _____

5. _____

6. _____

🔊 10.29 ¿Con quién habla? You will hear a guest at a hotel talking to her daughter, to the receptionist,
3-18 and to the bellboy. Listen to each one of her commands and decide to whom she is talking.

1. _____   **a.** su hija   **b.** el recepcionista   **c.** el botones

2. _____   **a.** su hija   **b.** el recepcionista   **c.** el botones

3. _____   **a.** su hija   **b.** el recepcionista   **c.** el botones

4. _____   **a.** su hija   **b.** el recepcionista   **c.** el botones

5. _____   **a.** su hija   **b.** el recepcionista   **c.** el botones

6. _____   **a.** su hija   **b.** el recepcionista   **c.** el botones

🔊 10.30 De vacaciones You will hear a conversation between two friends. Listen carefully and select the
3-19 correct answer.

1. _____ ¿Adónde viajaron Marisol y Rodolfo?

a. Puerto Rico   **b.** Costa Rica   **c.** la República Dominicana

2. _____ ¿Por cuánto tiempo estuvieron de viaje?

a. un fin de semana   **b.** siete días   **c.** un mes

3. _____ ¿Qué tiene el Hotel Arenal?

a. una sauna y una piscina   **b.** una piscina y un gimnasio   **c.** una sauna y un gimnasio

4. _____ ¿Cuanto costó la habitación?

a. 1.240 colones   **b.** 53.000 colones   **c.** 1.350 colones

¡Hora de reciclar! 2

10.31 **¡A emparejar!** Match each description in column A with the most logical reaction in column B.

A	**B**
1. _____ Usted no pudo encontrar su pase de abordar.	**a.** Me puse furiosa.
2. _____ Yo no conocía a nadie en la fiesta.	**b.** Te pusiste avergonzada.
3. _____ Supiste que tu abuela estaba en el hospital.	**c.** Se alegró.
4. _____ Carlota me dijo que vio a mi novio con otra chica.	**d.** Se frustraban.
5. _____ Pudo estacionarse muy cerca de la plaza.	**e.** Te asustaste.
6. _____ Los peatones no podían cruzar el puente por la construcción que había.	**f.** Se puso nervioso.
7. _____ Tropezaste en la acera.	**g.** Me sentía tímido.

10.32 **El pretérito y el imperfecto 2** Complete the following paragraph with the appropriate form of the preterite or imperfect of the verb in parentheses.

El mes pasado mis amigos y yo (1.) _____ (ir) de vacaciones y yo (2.) _____

(hacer) la reservación del hotel. Cuando nosotros (3.) _____ (llegar), el recepcionista nos

(4.) _____ (decir) que no (5.) _____ (haber) ninguna reservación a mi nombre y

que todas las habitaciones (6.) _____ (estar) ocupadas. ¡Yo (7.) _____ (ponerse)

furioso! Él (8.) _____ (disculparse – *to apologize*) y (9.) _____ (recomendar) un

hotel que (10.) _____ (estar) muy cerca. ¡Afortunadamente ese hotel (11.) _____

(tener) varias habitaciones disponibles y (12.) _____ (quedarse) allí!

CAPÍTULO 11 ¿Es la moda arte?

Prueba tu vocabulario 1

11.1 **Diseños** Match the shirt to the description.

1. _____ Es una camiseta a rayas. **a.**

2. _____ Es una camiseta con estampado de flores. **b.**

3. _____ Es una camiseta lisa. **c.**

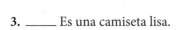

4. _____ Es una camiseta a cuadros. **d.**

5. _____ Es una camiseta de lunares. **e.**

11.2 **No corresponde** Circle the word that does not belong to each group.

1. rebajado   mediano   chico   grande

2. tarjeta de crédito efectivo   probador   caja

3. a rayas   de lunares   lino   estampado

4. talla   lana   mezclilla   algodón

5. elegante   bonito   lindo   apretado

6. caro   barato   rebajado   liso

11.3 **De compras** Select the most logical answer for each question.

1. ¿En qué puedo ayudarlo?
   a. Me quedan bien.
   b. Estoy buscando zapatos para niños.

2. ¿Quiere probarse la falda?
   a. Sí, ¿dónde están los probadores?
   b. Sí, ¿dónde puedo pagar?

3. ¿Cómo le queda el traje?
   a. ¡Qué caro!
   b. Voy a necesitar una talla más grande.

4. ¿Cómo desea pagar?
   a. En la caja.
   b. ¿Aceptan cheques?

5. ¿De qué tela son esas camisas?
   a. Son de algodón.
   b. Están rebajadas.

11.4 **Asociaciones** Choose four words from the first column and match each one with a word from the second column. Then write four sentences explaining the relationship between the word pairs.

algodón	caro
seda	ropa interior
caja	barato
piel	efectivo
rebajado	bolsa

1. _____

2. _____

3. _____

4. _____

Prueba tu gramática 1 y 2

Passive *se* and impersonal *se*

11.5 **Consejos para cuidar la ropa** Read the advice on how to ensure the long life of clothing, and complete the sentences with the appropiate form of the impersonal **se** and the passive **se.**

1. La ropa _____ (lavar) en agua fría y _____ (separar) las prendas blancas de las de color.

2. Para no tener arrugas *(wrinkles)* _____ (sacar) las prendas de la secadora inmediatamente y _____ (colgar).

3. Los suéteres nunca _____ (poner) en una secadora; _____ (secar) al aire.

4. Si es posible, _____ (recomendar) no usar la secadora.

5. Las blusas de seda _____ (poder) lavar a mano con agua fría.

6. Una chaqueta de piel _____ (deber) mandar a lavar con un profesional una vez al año.

11.6 **Cómo gastar menos en ropa** Using the passive **se,** write out the suggestions for buying clothing on a budget.

1. buscar / las ofertas / en las tiendas

_____

2. conseguir / prendas clásicas que siempre están a la moda

_____

3. ir / a las tiendas de ropa usada

_____

4. no utilizar / la tarjeta de crédito para pagar

_____

5. comprar / ropa de calidad

_____

11.7 **¿Qué se hace?** Write six original sentences explaining an activity that one does in the following places. Use the passive **se** and the impersonal **se**.

Modelo en la casa *Se lleva ropa cómoda.*

1. en la tienda de ropa _____

2. en el probador _____

3. en la caja _____

4. en el armario _____

5. enfrente del espejo _____

6. en la lavandería *(laundromat)* _____

Comparisons

11.8 **Diferencias** Read the descriptions and then complete the comparative statements with **más**, **menos**, and **que.**

1. Las botas cuestan $100 y los zapatos cuestan $90.
   a. Las botas cuestan _____ _____ los zapatos.
   b. Los zapatos cuestan _____ _____ las botas.

2. Elsa compró 4 camisas y su hermano Alex compró 2.
   a. Elsa compró _____ camisas _____ su hermano.
   b. Alex compró _____ camisas _____ su hermana.

3. La camisa de seda cuesta $75 y la camisa de algodón cuesta $50.
   a. La camisa de seda es _____ económica _____ la camisa de algodón.
   b. La camisa de algodón es _____ económica _____ la camisa de seda.

4. La camiseta roja es de talla mediana y la camiseta azul es de talla extra grande.
   a. La camiseta roja es _____ pequeña _____ la camiseta azul.
   b. La camiseta azul es _____ grande _____ la camiseta roja.

11.9 **Son iguales** Irma and Alma are twins and have a lot in common. Complete the comparisons of equality using the words **tan, tanto(s),** or **tanta(s)** and **como.**

1. Irma tiene _____ tarjetas de crédito _____ Alma.

2. Irma va de compras _____ _____ Alma.

3. La ropa que Irma compra es _____ cara _____ la ropa que compra Alma.

4. Alma gasta *(to spend)* _____ dinero en ropa _____ Irma.

5. Irma lleva zapatos _____ modernos _____ los de Alma.

11.10 **Dos amigas** Look at the drawings of Mónica and Irina. Compare the items of clothing they are wearing, using expressions of comparison.

1. (blusa) _____

_____

2. (sombrero) _____

_____

3. (falda) _____

_____

4. (bolsa) _____

_____

5. (botas) _____

_____

Mónica   Irina

© Cengage Learning®

11.11 **Opiniones** Saúl is very particular about what he wears. Using the elements indicated, write sentences to express his opinions with a superlative. **¡OJO!** Pay attention to the form and the placement of the adjectives.

   Modelo   Casa Lucas / tienda / elegante
   Casa Lucas es la tienda más elegante.

1. el algodón / tela / cómodo

_____

2. una camisa lisa / estilo / profesional

_____

3. la tarjeta de crédito / forma de pagar / bueno

_____

4. los zapatos de piel / zapatos / caro

_____

5. la tienda Gangas / tienda / malo

_____

¡Hora de escuchar! 1

🔊 **11.12** **¿Cuál es?** You will hear six descriptions. Listen carefully and decide to which drawing each
4-2 description refers.

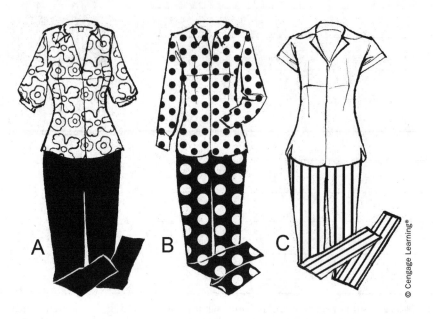

1. _____ 2. _____ 3. _____ 4. _____ 5. _____ 6. _____

🔊 **11.13** **¿Cierto o falso?** Listen to the conversation and indicate whether the statements are true
4-3 **(cierto)** or false **(falso)**.

1. Cierto   Falso   La señorita busca un vestido.

2. Cierto   Falso   Ella quiere una falda blanca en talla chica.

3. Cierto   Falso   El vestido negro que tiene el dependiente está rebajado.

4. Cierto   Falso   El vestido cuesta tanto como la falda.

5. Cierto   Falso   La señorita desea probarse la falda.

🔊 **11.14** **Comentarios** Listen to the comments made by different people shopping for clothing and decide
4-4 which word best completes each statement.

1. _____ cuestan más.   **a.** Las blusas   **b.** Los zapatos

2. El vestido _____ es más corto.   **a.** negro   **b.** rojo

3. Él necesita zapatos más _____.   **a.** pequeños   **b.** grandes

4. Para esta persona la calidad es _____ importante que el precio.   **a.** más   **b.** menos

---

¡Hora de reciclar! 1

11.15 **Los pronombres relativos** Create more sophisticated sentences by combining the sentences and using the pronouns **donde, que,** and **quien(es).**

Modelo Las botas altas son las mejores. Vi las botas en la tienda Zona Moda.
Las botas altas que vi en la tienda Zona Moda son las mejores.

1. El dependiente me va a ayudar a encontrar un traje. Hablé con él.

_____

2. La blusa estampada cuesta $25. La blusa estampada está rebajada.

_____

3. La tienda está cerrada hoy. Prefiero comprar mi ropa en esa tienda.

_____

4. Ella va a probarse el vestido rojo. El dependiente le trajo el vestido rojo.

_____

5. El señor es un empleado de la tienda. Él está en la sección de zapatos.

_____

11.16 **Los mandatos formales y de *nosotros*** Write the necessary commands for the following situations. You will have to decide whether to use **tú, usted, ustedes,** or **nosotros** commands.

1. Una amiga quiere comprar una blusa, pero no tiene efectivo.

No _____ (comprar) la blusa ahora.

_____ (Esperar) a verla rebajada.

2. Dos amigos quieren comprar ropa cómoda.

_____ (Probarse) la ropa antes de comprarla.

No _____ (usar) ropa de materiales sintéticos.

3. La madre de un amigo necesita un vestido para una boda, pero no tiene mucho dinero.

_____ (Buscar) vestidos rebajados.

No _____ (gastar) mucho dinero en un vestido que no va a usar mucho.

4. Un amigo quiere ir de compras contigo.

_____ (Ver) la ropa en la tienda Ropa, Ropa, Ropa porque tienen buenas rebajas hoy.

No _____ (ir) a la tienda Colorido porque no tienen ropa bonita.

¡Hora de escribir!

A student from Spain is going to be attending classes with you next semester and has e-mailed you asking about clothing. Answer the e-mail describing what students typically wear at your university and where students shop locally.

Paso 1 Jot down some general trends among students at your school. Are brand names or specific designers important? What do students generally wear to class as well as when they go out? Think about details: footwear, accessories, etc.

Paso 2 Jot down a list of local places where students tend to shop for clothing, as well as your preferred store. Write down some details about the store you prefer to shop in: Why do you like to shop there? What type of clothing do they have? Do they carry expensive clothing or shoes? How does the store, clothing, prices, etc. compare with those of other stores? How can one pay for items?

Paso 3 Write a greeting to your Spanish friend and ask what he/she normally wears. Describe some of the general trends at your school that you generated in **Paso 1.**

Paso 4 Look at the information you generated in **Paso 2** and begin a second paragraph telling him/her where students generally shop. Mention one of the stores you prefer to shop in and give details using the ideas from **Paso 2.** Be sure to include a few comparisons.

Paso 5 Write a conclusion to your e-mail and sign your name.

Paso 6 Edit your e-mail:

1. Do you have smooth transitions between sentences? Between the two paragraphs?
2. Do verbs agree with the subject?
3. Do adjectives agree with the items they describe?
4. Did you use comparative forms appropriately?

_____

_____

_____

_____

_____

_____

_____

_____

_____

_____

Prueba tu vocabulario 2

11.17 **¿Qué es?** Complete the sentences with a word from the vocabulary.

1. Una _____ tiene todos los colores que el pintor necesita para pintar un óleo.

2. El escultor esculpe una _____.

3. La _____ es un tipo de pintura que generalmente representa fruta y flores.

4. El _____ es un tipo de arte que es revolucionario y moderno.

5. Una pintura que muestra la cara de una persona es un _____.

6. Al pintar un cuadro, el pintor usa un _____ para pintar en el óleo.

11.18 **Estilos** Match each painting to the style it represents.

1. _____ retrato

2. _____ arte abstracto

3. _____ arte surrealista

4. _____ paisaje

5. _____ naturaleza muerta

a.

b.

c.

d.

e.

11.19 **Definiciones** Match each definition with a word from the second column.

1. _____ Arte tradicional que puede cubrir la cara de una persona.　　**a.** modelo

2. _____ Es el tipo de arte que hace un escultor.　　**b.** sencillo

3. _____ Un estilo de arte que es lo opuesto de realista.　　**c.** máscara

4. _____ Es lo contrario de **complicado**.　　**d.** exhibición

5. _____ Es la persona que posa para un artista.　　**e.** esculturas

6. _____ Es un evento en el que se muestra el arte de un artista.　　**f.** abstracto

---

11.20 **No pertenece** Choose the word in each list that does not belong.

1. impresionista　　surrealista　　cubista　　extraño

2. la máscara　　el modelo　　la escultura　　el grabado

3. el paisaje　　la paleta　　el pincel　　la tinta

4. diseñar　　esculpir　　posar　　pintar

11.21 **Identificaciones** Match a word from the first group with a verb from the second group, and write a sentence using both words.

Grupo 1: el grabado　　el modelo　　el paisaje　　la galería　　el mural　　el retrato

Grupo 2: diseñar　　exhibir　　esculpir　　trazar　　posar　　apreciar　　acabar

1. _____

2. _____

3. _____

4. _____

5. _____

Prueba tu gramática 3 y 4

Estar with the past participle

11.22 **Una mala idea** Complete the paragraph with the correct past participle form of the appropriate verb. ¡OJO! One verb will not be used.

abrir　　cerrar　　colgar　　encerrar　　hacer　　morir　　romper

Cuando Federico llegó, la galería estaba (1.) _____, pero él necesitaba tomar fotos, así que entró

por una ventana que estaba (2.) _____. La alarma de la galería sonó y Federico se asustó mucho.

Rápidamente tomó fotografías de unos cuadros que estaban (3.) _____ en la pared, pero cuando

terminó de tomar las fotos, la policía llegó. Federico se tiró al suelo (*threw himself to the ground*) y fingió

(*pretended*) estar (4.) _____. Esta idea no funcionó bien porque al caer al suelo su cámara fotográfica

quedó (5.) _____. Además, Federico estuvo (6.) _____ en la cárcel (*jail*) por una semana.

11.23 **Las descripciones** Describe the condition of the following things, using **estar** and the past participle of the underlined verb. Follow the model.

Modelo El modelo <u>murió</u>. El modelo *está muerto.*

1. El artista <u>se despertó</u>. El artista _____.

2. El pintor <u>vendió</u> los cuadros. Los cuadros _____.

3. La escultora <u>terminó</u> la escultura. La escultura _____.

4. El fotógrafo <u>rompió</u> unas fotos. Las fotos _____.

5. El diseñador <u>hizo</u> un diseño moderno. El diseño _____.

6. El artista <u>escribió</u> un anuncio para su exhibición. El anuncio _____.

11.24 **El estudio** Using the verb **estar** and the past participle, write five sentences to describe the picture below.

Vocabulario útil: **la cerámica**

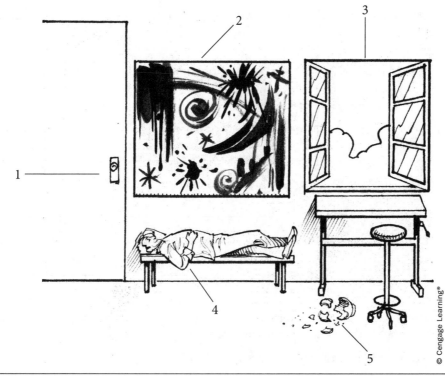

© Cengage Learning®

1. _____

2. _____

3. _____

4. _____

5. _____

Se to indicate accidental occurrences

11.25 **Algunos problemas** Complete the statements with the accidental **se** and the correct preterite form of the verb in parentheses.

1. A los estudiantes _____ (acabar) el tiempo para terminar el proyecto.

2. A nosotros _____ (perder) las máscaras.

3. Al escultor _____ (caer) la escultura.

4. A mí _____ (quedar) las entradas para la exposición en casa.

5. A ti _____ (olvidar) que la exposición es hoy.

6. A los artistas _____ (apagar) las luces.

11.26 **Distraídos** Using the accidental **se** and phrases in parentheses write sentences indicating what happened to these people.

Modelo La galería está cerrada. (el artista / olvidar abrir la galería)
Al artista se le olvidó abrir la galería.

1. El estudiante de arte no compró sus libros. (estudiante / perder su tarjeta de crédito) _____

_____

2. Todas las máscaras están rotas. (el artista / romper las máscaras) _____

_____

3. Los artistas no llegaron a la galería a tiempo. (los artistas / descomponer el auto) _____

_____

4. Las esculturas no están en la galería. (el artista / quedar las esculturas en su estudio) _____

_____

5. Los pintores no terminaron el mural. (los pintores / acabar las pinturas) _____

_____

11.27 **¡Qué barbaridad!** Choose the verb from the list that makes the most sense for each accident, and use it to complete the sentences logically. Use each verb only once.

acabar   **caer**   **descomponer**   **olvidar**   **perder**   **quedar**

1. La modelo no pudo vestirse porque _____ los pantalones.

2. Los estudiantes no pudieron terminar su tarea porque _____ la computadora.

3. No pude abrir la puerta de mi coche porque _____ las llaves adentro.

4. El profesor de arte no pudo tomar fotos de las obras de sus estudiantes porque _____ cómo usar su nueva cámara digital.

5. La escultura está rota porque al artista _____ la pieza.

¡Hora de escuchar! 2

 11.28 **Varios artistas** You will hear several statements about the paintings below. Listen carefully, decide to which picture each statement refers, and write the corresponding letter in the space provided.

a.

b.

c.

1. _____ 2. _____ 3. _____ 4. _____ 5. _____

11.29 **¿Qué le pasó?** Listen to four people tell what happened to them and decide which of the statements best summarizes the incident.

1. **a.** Se le descompuso el auto.   **b.** Se le acabó la gasolina.

2. **a.** Se le rompió un plato.   **b.** Se le quedó el dinero en casa.

3. **a.** Se le descompuso la computadora. **b.** Se le olvidó el ensayo.

4. **a.** Se les cayeron las luces.   **b.** Se les apagaron las luces.

11.30 🔊 **Francisco de Goya y Lucientes** Listen to the information about a famous Spanish painter.
4-7 Then, choose the correct answer to the following questions.

1. ¿Cuál era el tema de las primeras obras de Goya?
   a. arte religioso   **b.** retratos de personas ricas   **c.** arte abstracto

2. ¿Qué pasó en 1792?
   a. Se casó.   **b.** Se enfermó.   **c.** Tuvo su primera exhibición.

3. ¿Qué significa la palabra *sordo*?
   a. No puede oír.   **b.** No puede hablar.   **c.** No puede ver.

4. ¿Qué es el "período negro" de la obra de Goya?
   a. Pintaba con colores obscuros.   **b.** Pintaba escenas violentas.   **c.** No pintaba.

5. ¿Dónde murió Goya?
   a. en España   **b.** en Italia   **c.** en Francia

¡Hora de reciclar! 2

11.31 **Los mandatos informales** An artist has hired a young assistant to help her in the studio. Match each situation with the logical command that she might give the assistant. Then write the correct informal (**tú**) command form.

1. _____ Ella va a comenzar a pintar.

2. _____ Quiere hacer un retrato.

3. _____ Quiere mucha luz para ver bien.

4. _____ Necesita silencio para concentrarse.

5. _____ Terminó de pintar por el día.

6. _____ Quiere exhibir sus nuevas obras.

a. _____ (Recoger) las pinturas.

b. No _____ (hablar) mientras trabajo.

c. _____ (Llamar) a la modelo.

d. _____ (Traer) la paleta y los pinceles.

e. _____ (Contactar) la galería.

f. No _____ (cerrar) las cortinas.

11.32 **Los mandatos con pronombres** An artist is telling the people around him what he wants done. Write the commands he uses, choosing the proper form (**tú, usted,** or **ustedes**).

1. a su modelo (no moverse) _____

2. a su agente (buscarme nuevos clientes) _____

3. a los estudiantes de su clase (dibujarse) _____

4. a sus admiradores (no olvidarse de asistir a mi exposición) _____

5. a su perro (no molestarme ahora) _____

CAPÍTULO 12 ¿Qué será de nuestro planeta?

Prueba tu vocabulario 1

12.1 **¿Qué es?** Complete the statements with a logical vocabulary word.

1. En las playas hay _____; puede ser blanca, amarilla o negra.

2. El _____ es un lugar con muchos árboles, pero no es tropical.

3. En un _____ llueve muy poco.

4. Una _____ está rodeada de agua por tres lados y está conectada a tierra por un lado.

5. Los _____ llevan agua al mar. El segundo más largo del mundo es el Amazonas.

6. La _____ es un tipo de planta que crece en los trópicos. Sus frutos son cocos o plátanos.

7. Las vemos en el mar y el viento las produce. Necesitamos las _____ para surfear.

8. Las _____ que traen la lluvia están en el cielo.

12.2 **Asociaciones** Match each of the following nouns with the statement that best describes it.

la bahía   **el bosque**   **el esmog**   **el medio ambiente**   **el río**   **el volcán**

1. _____ Hace erupción y produce gases peligrosos.

2. _____ Es un lugar donde el mar está tranquilo.

3. _____ Es afectado por la deforestación.

4. _____ Trae agua a toda la región.

5. _____ Es todo lo que hay a nuestro alrededor.

6. _____ Contamina nuestro aire.

12.3 **El medio ambiente** Read the statements carefully and decide if they are true (**cierto**) or false (**falso**). For any false statements, change the underlined word to another word from the vocabulary that would make the statement true.

Modelo   Cierto (Falso) Puedo surfear en <u>la isla</u>.
<u>las olas</u>

1. Cierto   Falso   Se puede escalar en <u>los ríos</u>.

_____

2. Cierto   Falso   En el desierto hay <u>cactus</u>.

_____

3. Cierto   Falso   La palmera es un tipo de <u>pasto</u> que da frutos como cocos y plátanos.

_____

4. Cierto   Falso   El petróleo es un <u>recurso natural</u> importante para la economía.

_____

5. Cierto   Falso   Los desechos industriales <u>preservan</u> nuestro medio ambiente.

_____

6. Cierto   Falso   <u>El reciclaje</u> es una forma de proteger la naturaleza.

_____

12.4 **Diferencias** Write a sentence explaining the difference between the concepts in each word pair.

1. selva / bosque _____

_____

2. colina / montaña _____

_____

3. península / isla _____

_____

4. lago / mar _____

_____

5. contaminación / esmog _____

_____

Prueba tu gramática 1 y 2

Future tense

12.5 **Nuestro planeta** A scientist is making predictions about what will happen to our planet in the future. Complete the sentences using the correct future tense form of the appropriate verb from the list. Use each verb only once.

acabarse   **encontrar**   **extinguirse**   **haber**   **permitir**   **ser**   **tener**

Si el hombre continúa usando los recursos naturales sin medida, en el futuro cercano (1.) _____

las tierras de cultivo. Sin duda, (2.) _____ menos espacio disponible para cultivar, pues las

ciudades (3.) _____ más grandes que ahora y nuestro planeta (4.) _____ muchos

más habitantes. Desafortunadamente, muchas especies (5.) _____. Pero también es posible que

haya cambios positivos: probablemente los científicos (6.) _____ una cura para el cáncer y otras

enfermedades y la tecnología nos (7.) _____ viajar a lugares tan lejanos como la Luna *(Moon)* en

cuestión de algunas horas.

12.6 **Mi futuro** Using the verbs indicated, complete the statements of the following university students, who are saying what they think life will be like for them in five years.

1. ADRIANA: Dentro de cinco años yo _____ (tener) un buen trabajo.

2. BERTA: En cinco años yo _____ (estar) casada.

3. CARLOS: Yo _____ (ahorrar) mucho y _____ (poder) viajar por el mundo.

4. DIANA: Mi esposo y yo _____ (vivir) en Costa Rica, donde _____ (trabajar)

para proteger las reservas ecológicas.

5. ENRIQUE: Estoy seguro de que todos ustedes _____ (conseguir) cumplir sus sueños.

12.7 **¿Qué harán?** Based on where they are, indicate what the following people might be doing. Write complete sentences and use the future tense of **estar** and the present participle.

Modelo   Luisa está en la playa. (tomar el sol)   *Estará tomando el sol.*

1. José y Pablo están en las montañas. (escalar) _____

2. Mis primos están en un lago. (pescar) _____

3. Eva está en un volcán activo. (tomar fotos) _____

4. Estás en una isla desierta. (buscar agua potable) _____

5. Ustedes están en las nubes. (viajar en avión) _____

6. Gabriel está en las pampas argentinas. (montar a caballo) _____

7. Los muchachos están en la selva. (observar a los animales) _____

8. Estás entre las palmeras. (cortar cocos) _____

12.8 **Una campaña** Some university students began a campaign to raise awareness about the need to be more ecologically responsible. Complete the ideas on their flyer with the appropriate form of the future tense.

Si no actuamos ahora,...

1. ...nosotros _____ (destruir) el planeta y no _____ (tener) donde vivir.

2. ..._____ (haber) menos agua y muchas personas _____ (vivir) en zonas sin

   acceso al agua.

3. ...los ríos _____ (estar) contaminados y los peces _____ (morir).

4. ...la tierra _____ (quedarse) sin nutrientes y los agricultores no _____ (poder)

   cultivarla.

5. ..._____ (ser) demasiado tarde y nosotros no _____ (saber) cómo solucionar el

   problema.

Present perfect

12.9 **Este año** It is New Year's Eve, and Ricardo is reflecting on all of the things he has done over the last year. Complete the paragraph using the present perfect.

Este año (1.) _____ (ser) muy bueno para mí. Mis amigos y yo (2.) _____ (hacer)

varios viajes. Además, yo (3.) _____ (conseguir) un nuevo trabajo y mi novia

(4.) _____ (terminar) sus estudios en la universidad. Juntos mi novia y yo (5.) _____

(decidir) hacer más por el medio ambiente y nosotros (6.) _____ (empezar) a reciclar todo.

Gracias a nuestro reciclaje también (7.) _____ (ahorrar – *to save*) un poco de dinero, y con ese

dinero esperamos poder comprar bicicletas muy pronto para manejar menos.

12.10 **Un mensaje** Complete this e-mail message from a mother to her children with the correct present perfect form of the verb in parentheses.

Queridos hijos:

Llegué a Chile ayer por la mañana, así que todavía no (1.) _____ (hacer) mucho pero ya

(2.) _____ (escribir) una lista de todos los lugares que quiero ver en la ciudad de

Santiago. Hay muchos museos aquí y solo (3.) _____ (visitar) el Museo Histórico

Nacional. Yo (4.) _____ (decidir) ir al centro arqueológico de Pukará esta tarde.

Un guía del hotel me (5.) _____ (recomendar) ir a Viña del Mar para ver las hermosas

playas chilenas. Además (6.) _____ (comenzar) el festival de Viña del Mar. Todos me

(7.) _____ (decir) que es uno de los mejores festivales de música en español.

Mi amiga María todavía no (8.) _____ (llegar) de Rancagua, pero debe llegar pronto.

No la (9.) _____ (ver) en dos años y estoy muy emocionada de verla. Ella y yo

(10.) _____ (comprar) boletos para ir a la Isla de Pascua la próxima semana. ¡Voy a tomar

muchas fotos! Les escribo más desde allá.

Un beso,

Mamá

12.11 **Un viaje** Marcela, Pedro, and Román are going to travel to Venezuela to visit a national park. Combine the verb with the most logical phrase to tell what they have done to prepare for the trip.

Modelo conseguir – un pasaporte para viajar
Han conseguido un pasaporte para viajar.

1. hacer   información sobre Venezuela
2. hablar   un hotel
3. leer   boletos de avión
4. reservar   con personas que conocen Venezuela
5. comprar   las maletas con ropa apropiada

1. _____

2. _____

3. _____

4. _____

5. _____

12.12 **Este semestre** Using the present perfect, tell whether or not you have done the following things this semester. If you have, be sure to add some additional information.

> **Modelo**   dar una presentación
> *He dado una presentación en la clase de inglés. / No he dado una presentación este semestre.*

1. hacer un viaje _____

2. escribir una composición _____

3. romper algo _____

4. ver una buena película _____

5. decir una mentira _____

6. conocer a alguien _____

¡Hora de escuchar! 1

12.13 **Las definiciones** You will hear an explanation of a word from the vocabulary. Circle the word that is being described.

4-8

1. a. la pampa	**b.** la selva	**c.** el mar
2. a. la península	**b.** la isla	**c.** la bahía
3. a. el valle	**b.** el desierto	**c.** las colinas
4. a. el volcán	**b.** las montañas	**c.** el cielo
5. a. la arena	**b.** la ola	**c.** el mar
6. a. el pasto	**b.** el cielo	**c.** las nubes

12.14 **Preguntas** Choose the most logical answer to each question you will hear.

4-9

1. a. Iré en marzo.	**b.** Viajaré a Puerto Rico.	**c.** Tendré una semana de vacaciones.
2. a. Viajaré con una amiga.	**b.** Hablaré con el agente.	**c.** Pagaré con tarjeta de crédito.
3. a. Estaremos en un hotel en la playa.	**b.** Nos quedaremos una semana.	**c.** Visitaremos algunos lugares turísticos.
4. a. Nadaré en la playa.	**b.** Necesitaré vacaciones.	**c.** Haré mis maletas.
5. a. Iremos por tres días.	**b.** Saldremos mañana.	**c.** Volveremos la próxima semana.

🔊 **12.15** **Una entrevista de trabajo** Listen to Magdalena's interview and decide if the following
4-10   statements are true (**cierto**) or false (**falso**).

1. Cierto Falso La persona que tiene el trabajo tendrá que vivir en una gran ciudad.

2. Cierto Falso En el pasado Magdalena trabajó en una bahía.

3. Cierto Falso Magdalena es una persona aventurera.

4. Cierto Falso Ella estudiará en Puerto Rico y en España.

5. Cierto Falso No le dieron el trabajo a Magdalena.

¡Hora de reciclar! 1

12.16 **Se pasivo** Complete the statements to say what is done in an environmentally friendly household.

1. _____ (Reciclar) el papel y los plásticos.

2. La lavadora y el lavaplatos _____ (operar) solo cuando están llenos (*full*).

3. _____ (Donar) la ropa que ya no _____ (usar).

4. _____ (Apagar) las luces al salir (*when leaving*) de una habitación.

5. _____ (Comprar) los productos locales.

6. _____ (Caminar) o _____ (tomar) el autobús cuando es posible.

12.17 **Comparaciones** Complete each the following comparisons using **más, menos, tan,** or **tanto(s)/
tanta(s)**.

1. Un volcán es _____ peligroso que una colina.

2. En el desierto hay _____ animales que en la selva.

3. La costa es _____ bonita como las montañas.

4. Preservar nuestros recursos es _____ importante como reciclar.

5. Yo reciclo _____ como mis amigos.

6. Las palmeras no crecen en _____ lugares como los cactus.

¡Hora de escribir!

Write an email to a friend about a national park or a reserve that you will visit. If you have never been to a national park, find information about one on the Internet.

© Lysithee/Shutterstock

Paso 1 Jot down as many things about the park as you can. Think about the following questions: What is it like? Where is it? What can you see there? What can you do there? Is there something that makes it special? How is it being protected?

Paso 2 Think about a future visit to the park that you will make. Write down as many details as you can. Think about the following questions: When will you go? Who will you go with? What will you do there?

Paso 3 Greet your friend and ask if he or she ever visited a national park. Introduce your topic, mentioning the national park you plan to visit. Then using the present tense write your first paragraph giving the details about the park using some of the information you generated in **Paso 1.**

Paso 4 Write a transition sentence in which you introduce the topic of your visit to the park. Then, using the future tense and information you generated in **Paso 2,** develop your second paragraph telling what you plan to do. Be sure to write a concluding statement at the end of the second paragraph.

Paso 5 Edit your paragraph:

1. Do you have smooth transitions between sentences? Between the two paragraphs?
2. Do verbs agree with the subject?
3. Did you use the appropriate verb tense in each paragraph?
4. Do adjectives agree with the nouns they describe?

_____

_____

_____

_____

_____

_____

_____

_____

_____

_____

Prueba tu vocabulario 2

12.18 **El hábitat** Match the animals with the habitat where you would most likely find them. Choose only one letter for each number.

1. ____ el venado   **a.** el cielo

2. ____ el mono   **b.** el río

3. ____ el águila   **c.** el desierto

4. ____ la serpiente   **d.** el mar

5. ____ el cocodrilo   **e.** el bosque

6. ____ el tiburón   **f.** la selva

12.19 **No corresponde** Choose the animal that does not belong to each group.

1. **a.** el zorro   **b.** el venado   **c.** el oso   **d.** la jirafa

2. **a.** la rana   **b.** la gallina   **c.** el pato   **d.** el águila

3. **a.** el jaguar   **b.** la serpiente   **c.** el tigre   **d.** el león

4. **a.** la ballena   **b.** el elefante   **c.** el mono   **d.** el cocodrilo

5. **a.** la oveja   **b.** la vaca   **c.** el cerdo   **d.** el lobo

12.20 **Clasificaciones** Write the classification of each of the animals listed.

  anfibio **ave** **mamífero** **pez** **reptil**

1. el águila _____

2. la ardilla _____

3. la ballena _____

4. el cocodrilo _____

5. el conejo _____

6. la llama _____

7. la rana _____

8. la serpiente _____

9. la tortuga _____

10. el tiburón _____

12.21 **Identificaciones** Give the name of each animal that you see in the drawing. Be sure to include the definite article.

1. _____   6. _____

2. _____   7. _____

3. _____   8. _____

4. _____   9. _____

5. _____   10. _____

Prueba tu gramática 3 y 4

Subjunctive with impersonal expressions

12.22 **Es importante** Jacobo is going to work at the zoo. The following is a list of things that he must remember as he takes care of the animals. Write the correct form of the subjunctive in the spaces.

Es importante que…

1. los peces _____ (estar) en el agua.

2. los pingüinos _____ (tener) mucho hielo.

3. los leones no _____ (atacar) a las cebras.

4. el gorila no _____ (salirse) de su jaula.

5. los tigres _____ (comer) carne.

6. el oso no _____ (asustar) a los otros animales.

Nombre _____ Fecha _____

12.23 En el bosque Cristián y Ronaldo are planning a hike in the forest. Cristián makes some suggestions of what they might do. Complete Ronaldo's reactions using the subjunctive, as in the model.

Modelo —Vamos a buscar un oso. —No es buena idea que *busquemos un oso.*

1. —Vamos a jugar con las ardillas. —No es buena idea que _____.

2. —Vamos a cazar venados. —Es mala idea que _____.

3. —Vamos a nadar con los patos. —Es ridículo que _____.

4. —Vamos a correr con los lobos. —Es imposible que _____.

5. —Vamos a darles de comer a los zorros. —No es recomendable que _____.

12.24 La visita a la granja You are taking a group of small children to visit a farm. Complete the following statements with recommendations for the children.

1. Es buena idea que _____.

2. Es necesario que _____.

3. Es malo que _____.

4. Es posible que _____.

5. Es mejor que _____.

Subjunctive with expressions of doubt

12.25 ¿Subjuntivo? Read the following statements and decide if you need the subjunctive or not.

1. No es cierto que las vacas (son / sean) tontas.

2. Es evidente que los pingüinos (están / estén) en peligro de extinción.

3. No creo que los elefantes (saben / sepan) cantar.

4. No estamos seguros de que las ovejas (dan / den) la mejor lana.

5. Es obvio que los conejos (se reproducen / se reproduzcan) rápidamente.

6. Dudamos que (hay / haya) muchos jaguares en Norteamérica.

12.26 **Al acampar** Jorge and Elena are camping in the woods. Complete their conversation with the correct present indicative or subjunctive form of the verbs in parentheses.

ELENA: Jorge, creo que un animal (1.) _____ (estar) cerca de nuestra tienda.

JORGE: No creo que (2.) _____ (haber) nada. Pienso que tú (3.) _____ (tener) mucha imaginación.

ELENA: Dudo que (4.) _____ (ser) mi imaginación. Estoy segura de que (5.) _____ (escuchar) un animal. ¿No lo escuchas tú? Creo que (6.) _____ (ser) un oso.

JORGE: No, Elena, no pienso que los osos (7.) _____ (vivir) en esta parte del bosque. ¡Duérmete!

ELENA: No creo que yo (8.) _____ (poder) dormir. Estoy segura de que yo (9.) _____ (ver) una sombra *(shadow)* afuera.

JORGE: Bueno, voy a mirar, pero estoy seguro de que (10.) _____ (ser) solo el viento… ¡Ay! ¡Tienes razón! ¡Es un oso!

12.27 **En peligro** Using the elements given, write complete sentences. You will need to add **que** in the appropriate place. **¡OJO!** The initial expression will determine whether you need to use the present indicative or the present subjunctive.

Modelo   es obvio / los conejos / reproducirse / muy rápido
Es obvio que los conejos se reproducen muy rápido.

1. creo / los osos / ser / peligrosos

_____

2. no pienso / las vacas/ beber / leche

_____

3. es verdad / los tigres / estar / en peligro de extinción

_____

4. no es cierto / las ranas / vivir / en el mar

_____

5. dudo / las ovejas / poder / sobrevivir en el desierto

_____

12.28 **Oraciones incompletas** Complete the following statements. You will need to decide whether to use the present subjunctive or the present indicative.

1. Creo que los elefantes _____.

2. Dudo que las jirafas _____.

3. Es obvio que los cerdos _____.

4. No pienso que las tortugas _____.

5. No es cierto que las serpientes _____.

¡Hora de escuchar! 2

12.29 **¿Qué animal es?** You will hear descriptions of animals. For each description, choose the animal to which it refers.

1. **a.** el oso   **b.** la cebra   **c.** el tigre   **d.** el cerdo

2. **a.** las ranas   **b.** las ballenas   **c.** las ardillas   **d.** las águilas

3. **a.** la vaca   **b.** el gorila   **c.** la cebra   **d.** el zorro

4. **a.** el león   **b.** la serpiente   **c.** el mono   **d.** el lobo

5. **a.** los anfibios   **b.** los peces   **c.** los reptiles   **d.** los mamíferos

12.30 **¿Es posible?** Listen to the statements and decide whether they are possible or impossible. Then complete the sentences below.

Modelo   You hear: Las jirafas comen carne.
           You write: Es posible / (imposible) que *las jirafas coman carne.*

1. Es posible / imposible que _____.

2. Es posible / imposible que _____.

3. Es posible / imposible que _____.

4. Es posible / imposible que _____.

5. Es posible / imposible que _____.

🔊 **12.31** **Una especie en peligro** Listen to the information about an endangered animal and choose the
4-13 correct answer to each of the following questions.

1. ¿Por qué es conocido el tigre?   **a.** por ser feroz   **b.** por ser grande

2. ¿Para qué se usan partes de los tigres?   **a.** para hacer abrigos   **b.** para hacer medicinas

3. ¿Dónde está la mayoría de los tigres ahora?   **a.** en Bali y Java   **b.** en la India

4. ¿Cómo podemos ayudar a salvar al tigre?   **a.** Podemos mandarles   **b.** Podemos formar nuevas
                                               dinero a organizaciones.   organizaciones.

¡Hora de reciclar! 2

12.32 *Estar* **con participios** Write the correct past participle form of the verb in parentheses.

1. A las 3:00 de la mañana el granjero (*farmer*) ya está _____ (despertar) aunque (*although*) está

   _____ (cansar).

2. Cuando llega con las gallinas la puerta está _____ (abrir).

3. Él está _____ (preocupar) por las gallinas.

4. Cuando entra, él nota que ninguna gallina está _____ (morir) pero están _____

   (asustar).

5. Llegó a tiempo, pero supone que el zorro está _____ (esconder – *to hide*) esperando otra

   oportunidad.

12.33 **El se accidental** Rosa is having a bad day at the zoo. Using the accidental **se** and the verbs in
parentheses, explain what happened.

1. Llegó tarde al zoológico. _____ (Descomponer) el coche.

2. No puede abrir la puerta. _____ (Olvidar) las llaves.

3. No puede darles de comer a los pingüinos. _____ (Acabar) los peces.

4. Los chimpancés no están en su jaula. _____ (Escapar) cuando abrió la puerta.

5. No tiene nada para comer durante el almuerzo. _____ (Quedar) su sándwich en casa.

CAPÍTULO 13 ¿Es tu vida una telenovela?

Prueba tu vocabulario 1

13.1 **Crucigrama** Complete the crossword using the hints given below.

Horizontales

3. Es la acción de tocar con los labios.

6. Es una palabra para hablar de un evento como una boda o una graduación.

8. Es la parte de la vida cuando vamos a la escuela primaria.

Verticales

1. Es lo opuesto a la vida.

2. Es el período de la vida donde muchos jóvenes tienen su primera relación amorosa.

4. Es la fiesta que se hace después de una boda.

5. Es la acción de formalizar una relación entre dos personas que quieren casarse.

7. Es la acción de rodear con los brazos a otra persona.

13.2 **Ideas incompletas** Select the verb that completes each idea logically and then conjugate it in the appropriate tense (present or preterite) as needed. You may use each verb only once.

abrazar   **besar**   **nacer**   **odiar**   **querer**   **romper**

1. En muchos países los hombres no se besan, se _____ para saludarse.

2. A Guillermo y a Héctor no les gusta ir a eventos sociales y ellos _____ las bodas.

3. Magdalena _____ a su novio y después le dijo "Te _____".

4. Pedro _____ con Gisela y ahora ella está saliendo con otro chico.

5. Yo _____ en Bogotá, pero me crié en Medellín.

13.3 **Definiciones** Match the concepts with the explanations that apply to them.

1. _____ dar a luz

2. _____ la vejez

3. _____ la madrina

4. _____ el anillo de compromiso

5. _____ extrañar

a. Hace la promesa de ser parte de la vida de un niño.

b. Es la última parte de la vida.

c. Es un símbolo de amor que se da al comprometerse.

d. Tener nostalgia por alguien o algo.

e. Es cuando nace un niño.

13.4 **Relaciones** Select a word from the first column and match it to a word from the second column. Then write a sentence explaining the relationship between the two words.

prometido	nacimiento
luna de miel	romper
divorciarse	boda
estar embarazada	soltero
la cita	comprometerse

1. _____

2. _____

3. _____

4. _____

5. _____

Prueba tu gramática 1 y 2

Reciprocal verbs

13.5 **Acciones** Complete each sentence with the correct form of the appropriate reciprocal verb in parentheses. **¡OJO!** Pay attention to the tense of the verbs.

Modelo   Hugo y Marcela se encontraron en el aeropuerto y *se abrazaron*. (abrazarse / divorciarse)

1. Miguel le propuso matrimonio a Verónica. Ella dijo que sí y _____. (saludarse / besarse)

2. Mario y Sara estaban casados pero tenían problemas y decidieron _____.

   (llevarse / separarse)

3. Antes Víctor y Carolina eran novios, pero ahora _____. (odiarse / hablarse)

4. Mis padres _____ en 1980 en una parada de autobuses. (conocerse / llevarse)

5. Como muchos jóvenes hoy día, Valentina y Juanjo _____ mensajes de texto todos los días.

   (verse / escribirse)

6. Ernesto y yo somos buenos amigos; _____ con los problemas. (ayudarse / pelearse)

13.6 **El novio** Luci is telling her friends about her wonderful new boyfriend, Agustín. Complete her ideas using the correct form of the present indicative of the appropriate verb from the list.

abrazarse	encontrarse	llevarse bien	llamarse	tomarse	verse

¡Agustín es maravilloso! Él y yo (1.) _____ por teléfono todos los días. Además, desde que

(since) somos novios, nosotros (2.) _____ en algún café o en mi casa por las noches, por dos o

tres horas. Cuando caminamos por la calle (3.) _____ de la mano. Él también es un hombre muy

responsable. Tiene una hija pequeña y ellos (4.) _____ todos los fines de semana. Me encanta ver

cómo ellos (5.) _____ cuando se encuentran.

13.7 **Buenos amigos** Rephrase the following ideas about Mercedes and her friends. Use reciprocal constructions.

> **Modelo** Mercedes respeta a sus amigos y sus amigos la respetan.
> *Mercedes y sus amigos se respetan.*

1. Mercedes visita a sus amigos y sus amigos la visitan.

_____

2. Mercedes me invita a salir y yo la invito a ella.

_____

3. Los amigos de Mercedes la llaman por teléfono y ella los llama a ellos.

_____

4. Mercedes los saluda a ustedes con un beso. Ustedes también la saludan con un beso.

_____

5. Los amigos de Mercedes la entienden. Ella también los entiende.

_____

6. Yo me llevo bien con Mercedes y ella se lleva bien conmigo.

_____

13.8 **La boda** Complete the paragraph with the appropriate forms of the reciprocal verbs in parentheses. **¡OJO!** All but one of the verbs are in the preterite.

Mi novio y yo (1.) _____ (casarse) el año pasado y muchos de nuestros amigos asistieron

a nuestra boda. Mi amiga Rosa alguna vez fue novia de Arturo, otro de nuestros invitados, pero después

de que ellos (2.) _____ (pelearse) a causa de los celos de Rosa, ellos rompieron y no

(3.) _____ (hablarse) nunca más. ¡Mi novio y yo teníamos miedo de una pelea durante la boda!

Cuando Rosa y Arturo (4.) _____ (verse), ellos (5.) _____ (abrazarse) y

(6.) _____ (besarse). ¡Mi novio y yo nos sorprendimos mucho! Parece que ellos ya no

(7.) _____ (odiarse) y ahora son amigos otra vez.

Subjunctive with expressions of desire

13.9 **Deseos** Lili and Daniel just got engaged. They are talking about their plans for the future. Complete their conversation with the correct present subjunctive form or the infinitive of the verb in parentheses.

LILI: ¡Qué emoción! Quiero que nuestra boda (1.) _____ (ser) en la iglesia donde me bautizaron.

DANIEL: Está bien. Yo deseo que nuestros invitados lo (2.) _____ (pasar) de maravilla en nuestra recepción. Mis padres sugieren que nosotros (3.) _____ (hacer) la fiesta en un hotel de lujo que está en la playa.

LILI: Mi madre desea que nosotros (4.) _____ (tener) la fiesta en su casa, pero mi padre quiere que nosotros la (5.) _____ (dar) en su casa… ¿Qué hacemos?

DANIEL: Es nuestra boda. ¿Qué prefieres (6.) _____ (hacer) tú?

LILI: Quiero que (7.) _____ (alquilar) un salón cerca de la iglesia.

DANIEL: Me parece muy bien. ¿Se lo quieres (8.) _____ (decir) a nuestros padres o prefieres que se lo (9.) _____ (decir) yo?

13.10 **El nuevo bebé** Renata and Fausto just had a baby boy. Complete the sentences expressing the family and friends' hopes and wishes for the child. Remember to use the subjunctive.

Modelo los abuelos / desear / el bebé / ser feliz
Los abuelos desean que el bebé sea feliz.

1. Renata / querer / el bebé / estar sano

_____

2. el hermano de Fausto / esperar / el niño / jugar al fútbol

_____

3. Fausto / recomendar / su esposa / darle frutas orgánicas

_____

4. la hermana de Renata / sugerir / el bebé / dormir con sus padres

_____

5. el cura *(priest)* / insistir en / los padres / traer al niño / a la iglesia

_____

13.11 **En la recepción** The guests are toasting to the bride and groom. Match their wishes with the most logical conclusion and write out the remainder of the sentences, conjugating the verb in parentheses as appropriate.

a. inolvidable	**d.** un matrimonio muy feliz
b. todas las decisiones juntos	**e.** mucha alegría
c. sin hacer reservaciones	**f.** buen tiempo en el lugar donde van a pasar la luna de miel

1. ____ Emilio: Yo espero que ustedes (tener) _____.

2. ____ Rocío: Quiero que su viaje de luna de miel (ser) _____.

3. ____ Ernesto: Sugiero que ustedes (tomar) _____.

4. ____ Cora: Ojalá que el futuro les (traer) _____.

5. ____ Gerardo: No les recomiendo que (viajar) _____.

6. ____ Mireya: Ojalá (hacer) _____.

13.12 **Así lo deseamos** Complete the following sentences with the subjunctive.

1. Mis amigos quieren que yo _____.

2. Espero que mi profesor(a) de español _____.

3. Ojalá que mis compañeros de clase y yo _____.

4. Necesito que alguien _____.

5. Prefiero que mis amigos _____.

¡Hora de escuchar! 1

13.13 **Relaciones** You will hear several statements about personal relationships. For each one, circle the word or phrase that is being described.

4-14

1. el viudo   el novio   el recién casado

2. casarse   divorciarse   comprometerse

3. la madurez   la vejez   la niñez

4. abrazar   extrañar   romper

5. la unión libre   la luna de miel   la ceremonia

◀)) **13.14** **Esposos** Look at the drawing and write logical answers to the questions you hear.
4-15

© Cengage Learning®

1. _____

2. _____

3. _____

4. _____

◀)) **13.15** **Un relato personal** Listen to the story and choose the correct answers to the questions below.
4-16

1. ____ ¿Cuántos años tenían cuando se conocieron Sofía y Darío?

   a. veinte   **b.** veintinueve   **c.** diecinueve

2. ____ ¿Qué hicieron en su primera cita?

   a. Miraron una película.   **b.** Pasearon en un lago.   **c.** Bailaron a la luz de la luna.

3. ____ ¿Adónde se fueron a vivir después de la boda?

   a. a Nicaragua   **b.** a México   **c.** a Estados Unidos

4. ____ ¿Por qué no fue fácil la vida de casados al principio (*at the beginning*)?

   a. Sofía extrañaba a su   **b.** Darío no tenía trabajo.   **c.** Sofía salía demasiado con amigos.
       familia.

5. ____ ¿Cuándo empezó a hacer nuevos amigos Sofía?

   a. antes de la boda   **b.** después de que nació su   **c.** después de que nació su tercer hijo
                   primer hijo

¡Hora de reciclar! 1

13.16 **El futuro** Some students are discussing what the future holds for them. Complete their statements with the correct future tense form of the verb in parentheses.

DEDÉ: Yo (1.) _____ (terminar) mis estudios al final del semestre y mi novio y yo

(2.) _____ (casarse) e (3.) _____ (ir) a vivir a Puerto Rico,

donde viven nuestras familias.

CARLOS: Mi esposa y yo (4.) _____ (celebrar) nuestro aniversario de bodas

en junio. (Nosotros) (5.) _____ (hacer) un viaje a Costa Rica donde

(6.) _____ (quedarse) en un hotel cerca del volcán Arenal.

REGINA: Mi hijo (7.) _____ (nacer) en tres meses... Él (8.) _____

(ser) nuestro primer hijo. Sé que nuestras vidas (9.) _____ (cambiar) drásticamente

pero estoy segura de que (nosotros) (10.) _____ (estar) muy felices.

13.17 **El presente perfecto** Choose the most logical verb to complete each sentence and conjugate it in the present perfect.

casarse	comprometerse	divorciarse	enamorarse	nacer

1. Esteban y Dafne no _____; están viendo a un consejero para arreglar su

matrimonio.

2. Tu hija estaba embarazada ¿no? ¿_____ tu nieto?

3. ¿Alguna vez (tú) _____ de la persona equivocada?

4. Fabricio es soltero y nunca _____.

5. Marisela y Daniel ya _____ y piensan casarse este verano.

¡Hora de escribir!

Write a short article to appear in the social section of the newspaper telling of the engagement of the couple in the photograph.

© Jeff Thrower/Shutterstock

Paso 1 Jot down some ideas about them: who they are, where they live, how old they are, who their families are, where they went to school, etc.

Paso 2 Jot down some ideas as to the development of their relationship: when and how they met, when and where they got engaged, when they will get married, where they will go on their honeymoon, etc.

Paso 3 Begin your article announcing the engagement of the couple. Then using the information you generated in **Paso 1,** write a paragraph in which you introduce each of them.

Paso 4 Write a second paragraph in which you tell the details of their relationship using the information you generated in **Paso 2.** Be sure to include some reciprocal verbs.

Paso 5 Edit your article:

1. Is the information clearly organized in a logical sequence?
2. Did you include ample details?
3. Do adjectives agree with the person or object they describe?
4. Do verbs agree with the subject?
5. Did you use the preterite and imperfect accurately?

_____

_____

_____

_____

_____

_____

_____

_____

_____

_____

_____

_____

_____

_____

Prueba tu vocabulario 2

13.18 **¿Qué es?** Write the word from the vocabulary that completes each idea logically.

1. Necesito el _____ para escribir en la computadora.

2. Es muy cómodo cambiar canales en la televisión con el _____.

3. Para encontar información en el Internet, usamos un _____ como Google o Bing.

4. Las _____ en este cine son muy cómodas.

5. Los programas _____ se transmiten antes de la ocho de la noche y muchos son de dibujos animados.

6. El nombre para referirse a las personas que ven la televisión es "_____".

7. El _____ de este programa de radio es una persona muy inteligente.

8. En el _____ de las diez de la noche dijeron que hubo un accidente en la carretera.

13.19 **Categorías** Organize the words from the list in the appropriate categories. Some words may belong to more than one category.

el ratón   el buscador   la programación   las redes sociales   el conductor

la butaca   el canal   el anuncio   la clasificación   el locutor   el éxito de taquilla

el control remoto   hacer clic

EL CINE: _____

_____

LA TELEVISIÓN: _____

_____

LA COMPUTADORA: _____

_____

13.20 **Definiciones** Match the explanations with the concept each one describes.

1. ____ Se comen en el cine.

2. ____ Es la acción de escribirse simultáneamente por Internet.

3. ____ Es quien paga por transmitir comerciales en la tele.

4. ____ Es un aparato que nos permite escuchar música.

5. ____ Es una publicación con artículos y fotos.

6. ____ Es un programa para la audiencia infantil.

a. los audífonos

b. la revista

c. dibujos animados

d. el patrocinador

e. las golosinas

f. chatear

13.21 **Preguntas personales** Answer the questions in complete sentences using a wide variety of vocabulary.

1. ¿Qué tipo de programas de televisión prefieres?

_____

2. En tu opinión, ¿cómo debe ser una película para ser un éxito de taquilla?

_____

3. ¿Te gustan las telenovelas? ¿Por qué?

_____

4. ¿Pasas más tiempo viendo la televisión o en el Internet? ¿Por qué?

_____

5. ¿Prefieres ver películas en casa o en el cine? ¿Por qué?

_____

Prueba tu gramática 3 y 4

The subjunctive with expressions of emotion

13.22 **Películas** A group of friends are talking about their personal taste in movies. Complete their opinions with the correct subjunctive form of the verb in parentheses.

Luz: ¡Me encanta que (1.) _____ (haber) drama en una película!

Ricardo: A mí me molesta que los actores (2.) _____ (besarse).

Braulio: Me fascina que el final de la película (3.) _____ (ser) inesperado (*unexpected*).

Lourdes: A mí me aburre que los protagonistas (4.) _____ (chocar) o

(5.) _____ (tener) accidentes.

Enrique: Pues a mí no me molesta tanto la violencia, pero me preocupa que los niños

(6.) _____ (ver) escenas violentas.

Mary Ely: Me alegro de que los directores de Hollywood (7.) _____ (producir) más

documentales.

13.23 **La tecnología** Complete each of the statements with the appropriate form of the present subjunctive. Then select the answer that most closely agrees with your opinion, and then write a full sentence with it.

> **Modelo** Me molesta que la tecnología...
> (ser) muy cara
> *Me molesta que la tecnología sea muy cara.*

1. Me gusta que la tecnología...

 a. me _____ (permitir) trabajar más rápido

 b. me _____ (conectar) con mis amigos

 c. _____ (hacer) fácil enterarse de todo

 _____

2. Me sorprende que la tecnología...

 a. _____ (avanzar) tan rápidamente

 b. no les _____ (interesar) a algunas personas

 c. _____ (cambiar) cómo se relacionan las personas

 _____

3. Me molesta de la tecnología que...

 a. ya no _____ (haber) privacidad

 b. yo _____ (tener) que actualizarla *(update it)* todo el tiempo

 c. no siempre _____ (funcionar) cuando la necesito

 _____

4. Me da miedo de la tecnología que...

 a. sin ella nosotros no _____ (poder) sobrevivir

 b. algunas personas la _____ (usar) para hacer daño

 c. mi información personal _____ (estar) a la vista de todos

 _____

Nombre _____ Fecha _____

13.24 Reacciones Complete the sentences using the verbs indicated in the present indicative and the present subjunctive as in the model. **¡OJO!** Remember you will need to use the indirect object pronoun with the verbs of emotion.

Modelo   A mi madre *le gusta* (gustar) que yo *traiga* (traer) películas en DVD para ver en casa.

1. A mí _____ (alegrar) que mi actor favorito _____ (estar) en el programa.

2. A mi amigo y a mí _____ (sorprender) que el canal _____ (ir) a cancelar el programa.

3. A mis padres _____ (molestar) que la cablevisión _____ (costar) mucho.

4. A mis compañeros _____ (gustar) que nosotros _____ (poder) chatear para ayudarnos con la tarea.

5. A mi profesor de español _____ (encantar) que nosotros _____ (ver) películas en español.

6. ¿A ti _____ (aburrir) que _____ (haber) muchos anuncios comerciales?

13.25 La tele Write reactions to the following statements using verbs of emotion and the subjunctive.

Modelo   La mayoría de las casas tiene más de un televisor.
No me sorprende que la mayoría de las casas tenga más de un televisor.

1. Hay programas muy variados.

_____

2. El estadounidense típico mira la tele cinco horas al día.

_____

3. El 30% de la programación consiste en anuncios comerciales.

_____

4. Millones de estadounidenses son adictos a la televisión.

_____

5. En los Estados Unidos, 50% de la población prefiere alquilar películas en vez de ir al cine.

_____

6. El 40% de los estadounidenses mira la televisión mientras cena.

_____

The subjunctive with adjective clauses

13.26 **Entretenimiento** The Ruiz family is brainstorming activities for a long weekend with their extended family. Complete their ideas with the appropriate indicative or subjunctive form of the verb in parentheses.

1. Yo quiero ir a un hotel que _____ (estar) cerca de la playa.

2. Los niños quieren llevar DVDs que _____ (tener) dibujos animados.

3. Compramos unas revistas que se _____ (vender) en el puesto de periódico.

4. Los adolescentes van a llevar sus MP3 con la música que les _____ (gustar).

5. Podemos comer en un restaurante que _____ (servir) comida cubana.

6. Los abuelos dicen que quieren comida que no les _____ (hacer) daño *(make them sick)*.

13.27 **Preferencias** Complete these sentences in a logical manner choosing from the second column and write the remainder of the phrase conjugating the verb in the subjunctive.

a. de noticias	**b.** dar información	**c.** dibujos animados
d. muchos comerciales	**e.** diversión	**f.** olvidarme de mis problemas

1. ___ A los niños les gustan los programas que (tener) _____.

2. ___ Los adultos prefieren programas que (ser) _____.

3. ___ La gente quiere ver algo que le (ofrecer) _____.

4. ___ Cuando voy al cine, prefiero ver una película que me (hacer) _____.

5. ___ La mayoría de los televidentes busca canales que no (transmitir) _____.

6. ___ No sabemos mucho del Internet; necesitamos hablar con alguien que nos (poder)

_____.

13.28 **¿Qué vemos?** Rubén and Noelia are planning to watch TV together. Complete their conversation, using the present indicative or the present subjunctive of the verbs in parentheses.

RUBÉN: ¿Hay un programa que te (1.) _____ (interesar) ver?

NOELIA: No sé... ¿hay algo que no (2.) _____ (ser) muy violento? ¡Hay muchos programas en la tele hoy día que (3.) _____ (tener) mucha violencia!

RUBÉN: Hay un documental sobre los animales en peligro de extinción que (4.) _____ (poder) ser interesante.

NOELIA: No quiero ver nada serio esta noche. Prefiero algún programa que me (5.) _____ (divertir), como una comedia.

RUBÉN: No hay ningún programa que (6.) _____ (empezar) ahora, pero hay una comedia de Eugenio Derbez que (7.) _____ (comenzar) en media hora. ¿Qué piensas?

NOELIA: ¡Perfecto! Voy a preparar los sándwiches que te (8.) _____ (gustar) y podemos cenar mientras lo miramos.

13.29 **¿A quién conoces?** Answer the following questions affirmatively or negatively, as indicated. ¡OJO! Some sentences will require the present subjunctive and others the present indicative.

   Modelo   ¿Conoces a alguien que practique un deporte?
             No, *no conozco a nadie que practique un deporte.*

1. ¿Conoces a alguien que trabaje en un restaurante?

   Sí, _____.

2. ¿Conoces a alguien que sea de otro país?

   No, _____.

3. ¿Conoces a alguien que hable otro idioma?

   Sí, _____.

4. ¿Conoces a alguien que toque un instrumento musical?

   No, _____.

5. ¿Conoces a alguien que mire programas de concurso?

   Sí, _____.

¡Hora de escuchar! 2

🔊 **13.30** **¿Cuál es?** You will hear six descriptions. Decide to which drawing each one refers. If the
4-17 statement does not refer to any of the drawings, just write an X on the line.

A.    B.    C.

© Cengage Learning®

1. _____ 2. _____ 3. _____ 4. _____ 5. _____ 6. _____

🔊 **13.31** **¿Quién habla?** Listen to the comments and decide who is speaking in each case.
4-18

1. a. un locutor   **b.** un televidente

2. a. una locutora   **b.** una televidente

3. a. un locutor   **b.** un televidente

4. a. una locutora   **b.** una televidente

🔊 **13.32** **Un anuncio** Listen to the television announcement and answer the following questions.
4-19

1. ¿Para qué es el anuncio?

  a. televisión por satélite

  b. televisión por Internet

  c. televisión por cable

2. ¿Qué tipo de canales que ofrece la compañía menciona el locutor?

  a. películas y deportes

  b. noticiarios y concursos

  c. documentales y cocina

3. ¿Qué servicio especial hay para los padres de niños pequeños?

  a. un descuento en canales de dibujos animados

  b. control para bloquear canales

  c. un paquete familiar

4. ¿Qué recibes gratis *(free)* si ordenas este mes?

  a. un canal de películas

  b. un control remoto

  c. servicio por un año

¡Hora de reciclar! 2

13.33 **El subjuntivo 1** Guillermo is sharing his opinions about television and technology with his family. Choose the correct impersonal expression to complete each sentence logically and then conjugate the verb in parentheses, using the subjunctive.

1. Es _____ (raro / buena idea) que este canal no _____ (transmitir) el

   partido. Normalmente tienen todos los partidos del equipo.

2. Es _____ (una lástima / urgente) que yo _____ (comprar) una tableta

   nueva. Esta no puede mostrar programas de televisión por Internet.

3. Es _____ (terrible / justo) que el gobierno _____ (censurar) el programa.

   Debemos tener toda la información.

4. Es _____ (importante / ridículo) que nosotros _____ (saber) los detalles.

   Voy a mirar el noticiario.

5. Es _____ (mejor / malo) que los niños _____ (ver) demasiada televisión.

   Necesitan salir a jugar.

6. Es _____ (necesario / triste) que nosotros _____ (llegar) temprano al

   centro comercial para conseguir los descuentos en las nuevas tabletas.

13.34 **El subjuntivo 2** Complete these sentences in a logical manner. ¡OJO! Some sentences will take the present indicative and some the present subjunctive.

1. Estamos seguros de que la película _____ (comenzar) en una hora.

2. Dudo que te _____ (gustar) el programa.

3. Pienso que el conductor _____ (ser) muy bueno.

4. No creo que los actores _____ (tener) mucho talento.

5. No es evidente que la telenovela _____ (ir) a tener un final feliz.

6. Es obvio que los televidentes _____ (querer) otro tipo de programación.

CAPÍTULO 14 ¿Qué haces en una emergencia?

Prueba tu vocabulario 1

14.1 Preguntas y respuestas Miguel is at the doctor's office. Match the doctor's questions from the first column with Miguel's answers from the second column. You will not use all of the items in the second column.

1. _____ ¿Tiene problemas de insomnio?

2. _____ ¿Está mareado?

3. _____ ¿Tiene alergias a algún medicamento?

4. _____ ¿Qué medicinas está tomando?

5. _____ ¿Tiene dolor?

a. Sí, me duele mucho el pecho.

b. Estoy tomando gotas para alergias.

c. No, puedo dormir muy bien.

d. Sí, la penicilina me hace mal efecto.

e. Sí, no puedo mantener el equilibrio fácilmente.

f. Sí, necesito una vacuna.

14.2 No corresponde For each series of words, identify the word that doesn't belong.

1. el estornudo / la tos / la fractura

2. la receta médica / la gripe / la pastilla

3. el hueso / el corazón / el esqueleto

4. la obesidad / la curita / la diabetes

5. la salud / el hígado / el pulmón

6. cortarse / recuperarse / sangrar

14.3 **La palabra que falta** Complete the ideas with the most logical word. Remember to conjugate verbs.

alergia	cortada	cortarse	curita	diabetes	diarrea
estornudar	jarabe	náuseas	obesidad	recuperarse	tos

1. Susanita sufre de alergias. Cuando hay polen en el aire, _____ todo el tiempo.

2. Manolo tuvo una cirugía y ahora él _____ en el hospital.

3. ¿Te cortaste? Te voy a traer una _____ para que la pongas en la herida.

4. Cuando estaba embarazada sentía unas _____ horribles por las mañanas.

5. La obesidad puede traer otras enfermedades, como la _____.

6. Si tienes _____ puedes tomar este jarabe... ¡es muy bueno!

14.4 **En el hospital** Describe these scenes at the hospital using as many words from the vocabulary as you can. Write two complete sentences about each drawing.

1. _____

_____

_____

_____

_____

_____

2. _____

_____

_____

_____

_____

_____

3. _____

_____

_____

_____

_____

_____

© Cengage Learning®

Prueba tu gramática 1 y 2

Conditional

14.5 **Por favor** Complete the doctor's requests to a nurse. Use the third-person (**usted**) form of the conditional.

1. ¿Le _____ (poner) una inyección al paciente?

2. Por favor, ¿me _____ (traer) las radiografías del paciente?

3. Señorita, ¿_____ (llamar) a la farmacia?

4. ¿Le _____ (tomar) la presión al paciente?

5. ¿Me _____ (hacer) el favor de buscar unos vendajes?

6. Por favor, ¿_____ (poder) preparar las vacunas?

_____

14.6 **Enfermos** Read each situation and tell what each person would do. Use the conditional.

    Modelo   Lucrecia tiene la pierna rota. ¿Qué haría su médico?
              (ponerle un yeso) *Le pondría un yeso.*

1. Me duele la garganta. ¿Qué haría mi mamá?

(hacer una cita con el doctor) _____

2. Tu amigo tiene alergias. ¿Qué harías?

(recomendarle una medicina) _____

3. Tengo fiebre. ¿Qué harían mis amigos?

(traerte una aspirina) _____

4. Su hijo tiene un resfriado. ¿Qué haría usted?

(darle mucha agua) _____

5. Nosotros estamos mareados. ¿Qué haríamos nosotros?

(sentarse) _____

6. La abuela está respirando mal. ¿Qué haríamos todos?

(llevarla a la sala de emergencias) _____

14.7 **No hay límites** Carina's friend asked what she would do if she could do anything she wanted to and money and time were not an issue. Complete her statements using the conditional of the verbs indicated.

1. (Vivir) _____ en una isla.

2. No (trabajar) _____.

3. (Tener) _____ un chofer.

4. (Ser) _____ muy generosa.

5. (Ir) _____ al Caribe de vacaciones.

6. (Salir) _____ con mis amigos todas las noches.

7. (Comer) _____ en los restaurantes más famosos.

8. (Levantarse) _____ tarde todos los días.

14.8 **¿Qué pasaría?** Read each situation and use the conditional to write a conjecture about what might have been the circumstances.

> **Modelo**   La enfermera se desmayó. *¿Tendría miedo de la sangre?*

1. Me dolía el estómago. (tener un virus) ¿_____?

2. Estabas en la sala de emergencias. (sentirse enfermo) ¿_____?

3. Rocío tuvo un ataque al corazón. (sufrir de hipertensión) ¿_____?

4. Eva tenía náuseas. (estar embarazada) ¿_____?

5. Ellos estaban a dieta. (pensar que tenían sobrepeso) ¿_____?

6. Rogelio estaba en cama con fiebre, dolor y náuseas. (tener gripe) ¿_____?

Imperfect subjunctive

14.9 **Accidentes** The following people had accidents. Complete the recommendations, using the imperfect subjunctive of the verbs in parentheses.

1. Lolita se fracturó una pierna. Su médico le recomendó que _____ (descansar) por dos semanas. Su madre le sugirió que _____ (quedarse) con ella durante las dos semanas.

2. Mariano se desmayó. Su doctor le sugirió que _____ (trabajar) menos, y su jefe le ofreció que _____ (tomar) una semana de vacaciones.

3. El señor Costas se torció el tobillo. Su médico le dijo que _____ (recuperarse) completamente antes de volver a jugar al fútbol. También le recomendó que _____ (hacer) fisioterapia.

4. Valentina se cortó el dedo mientras cortaba el pan. Yo le recomendé que se lo _____ (lavar) con agua fría y que después _____ (ponerse) una curita.

5. Mi mejor amigo se cayó y se golpeó *(hit)* la cabeza. No le dolía, pero su mamá insistió en que _____ (ir) al médico y que le _____ (pedir) unas radiografías.

14.10 **Reacciones** Read the situations and write the appropriate form of the imperfect subjunctive of the verbs in parentheses.

1. El esposo de Alexis no quiso ir al médico. A Alexis le frustraba que su esposo no _____ (querer) ir.

2. Los hijos de Marianela estaban sanos. A Marianela le alegró que no _____ (enfermarse).

3. Mi amiga tuvo que caminar con muletas. Me preocupó que le _____ (doler) mucho.

4. La madre de Emilio tuvo que comprar medicamentos para él. A Emilio le molestó que su madre le _____ (dar) medicamentos.

5. La esposa de Benito estuvo mareada esta mañana. Benito esperaba que _____ (estar) embarazada.

6. Nuestro compañero tuvo una cirugía la semana pasada. Nos sorprendió que la cirugía _____ (durar) tres horas.

7. El padre de Beto tuvo un ataque al corazón. Beto temió que su padre _____ (morir).

8. Rafael tuvo gripe la semana pasada. A su equipo de fútbol no le gustó que no _____ (poder) jugar en el campeonato.

14.11 **Todos opinan** Felipe had the flu, and everyone gave him their advice. Using the elements given, write complete sentences telling what others recommended he do. ¡OJO! You will need to use **que** and conjugate the first verb in the preterite and the second verb in the imperfect subjunctive.

Modelo su mamá / decirle / tomar té
*Su mamá le **dijo** que **tomara** té.*

1. su mamá / pedirle / quedarse en cama

_____

2. su hermano / recomendarle / ir al médico

_____

3. su novia / decirle / tomar aspirina y caldo de pollo

_____

4. su mejor amigo / insistir en / beber muchos líquidos

_____

5. su jefe / mandarle / no trabajar

_____

6. su vecina / sugerirle / comer plátanos

_____

14.12 **Experiencias personales** Complete the ideas according to your own experiences using verbs in the imperfect subjunctive.

1. Una vez que me enfermé el doctor me sugirió que _____.

2. En mi último cumpleaños mis amigos me dijeron que _____.

3. En la escuela secundaria era importante que _____.

4. Yo me alegré de que un(a) amigo(a) _____.

5. Cuando era niño(a) no creía que _____.

6. Cuando decidí ir a la universidad busqué una universidad que _____.

14.13 **¿Qué harían?** Complete the following sentences with the appropriate forms of the imperfect subjunctive and the conditional of the verbs in parentheses.

1. Si yo _____ (tener) la presión alta _____ (comer) menos sal.

2. Mi esposo y yo _____ (cuidar) de mis padres si (ellos) _____ (estar) muy enfermos.

3. Si tú no _____ (seguir) los consejos del médico _____ (poder) tener serios problemas de salud.

4. Si no me _____ (gustar) mi médico (yo) _____ (buscar) otro.

5. Mi hermano _____ (saber) qué tiene si _____ (ir) a ver al médico.

6. Si tú _____ (tomar) el medicamento _____ (mejorarse) más rápido.

14.14 **¿Qué harías?** Complete the sentences expressing your own thoughts. You will need to use either the conditional or the imperfect subjunctive.

1. Si tuviera insomnio _____.

2. Tomaría una aspirina si _____.

3. Iría al hospital si _____.

4. Si no pudiera comprar los medicamentos _____.

5. Estaría muy preocupado si _____.

¡Hora de escuchar! 1

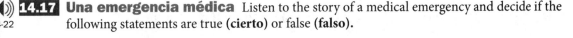

14.15 ¿Qué es? Listen to the description and circle the word in the list to which it applies.
4-20

1. la vacuna   la aspirina   el vendaje

2. la pastilla   la receta médica   el yeso

3. vomitar   desmayarse   recuperarse

4. las curitas   las gotas   la cirugía

5. la presión baja   el tratamiento   la salud

14.16 Síntomas Listen to the different people talk about their medical problems. Then decide what you
4-21   would logically do in each situation.

1. **a.** Me sentaría.   **b.** Me sentiría bien.

2. **a.** Tomaría aspirina.   **b.** Iría a la sala de emergencias.

3. **a.** Tendría que usar un yeso. **b.** Me pondría un vendaje.

4. **a.** Pediría radiografías.   **b.** Me fracturaría la pierna.

5. **a.** Haría más ejercicio.   **b.** Me tomaría la presión.

14.17 Una emergencia médica Listen to the story of a medical emergency and decide if the
4-22   following statements are true (**cierto**) or false (**falso**).

1. Cierto   Falso   El viernes pasado Alberto se sintió mal y no fue a trabajar.

2. Cierto   Falso   La esposa de Alberto insistió en que fuera a ver a un doctor.

3. Cierto   Falso   Un hombre se había tropezado en la calle.

4. Cierto   Falso   Alberto llamó una ambulancia.

5. Cierto   Falso   El hombre murió en el hospital después de dos horas.

6. Cierto   Falso   Alberto regresó a su casa muy enfermo.

¡Hora de reciclar! 1

14.18 **Los verbos recíprocos** Write at least two sentences for each of the drawings describing what the people are doing. ¡OJO! Use reciprocal verbs.

1.

1. _____

_____

_____

_____

_____

2.

2. _____

_____

_____

_____

_____

14.19 **Deseos** Complete the sentences with the verbs provided, using the present subjunctive, present indicative, or infinitive as needed.

1. Siempre le pido a mis padres que _____ (ir) al doctor una vez al año.

2. Mi mejor amigo quiere _____ (ser) enfermero, pero sus padres prefieren que él

_____ (estudiar) ingeniería.

3. Mis padres insisten en que mis hermanos y yo _____ (ponerse) gotas homeopáticas.

4. La doctora espera que sus pacientes _____ (seguir) sus recomendaciones.

5. Yo deseo _____ (aprender) primeros auxilios, pero mis amigos me recomiendan que

_____ (esperar) hasta el próximo año.

¡Hora de escribir!

Write an e-mail to a friend about a doctor's visit.

Paso 1 Jot down a list of illnesses or conditions for which someone might need to see a doctor. Then choose one and write down a list of symptoms that you associate with the particular illness or condition.

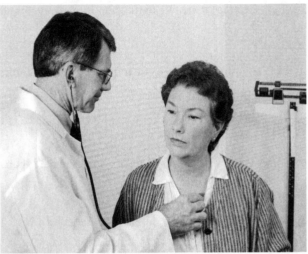

Paso 2 Jot down a list of tests that a doctor might do while examining you in his/her office as well as a list of recommendations he/she might make for the particular illness or condition.

Paso 3 Begin your e-mail by asking how your friend is feeling and then telling him/her that you have been feeling sick. Use the information you generated in **Paso 1** to describe what you have been experiencing.

Paso 4 Write a second paragraph telling your friend about your visit to the doctor's office using the information you generated in **Paso 2.** Be sure to include the doctor's diagnosis and recommendations.

Paso 5 Edit your e-mail:

1. Do you have smooth transitions between sentences and between paragraphs?
2. Do verbs agree with the subject?
3. Did you use the appropriate verb tense?
4. Did you use any expressions that require the subjunctive?

_____

_____

_____

_____

_____

_____

_____

_____

_____

_____

_____

_____

_____

_____

_____

Nombre ______________________________ Fecha ______________

Prueba tu vocabulario 2

14.20 Crucigrama Read the definitions and complete the crossword puzzle.

Vertical

1. Es el fenómeno que hace que todos los países se interrelacionen.

4. Es lo opuesto a la paz.

5. Es una persona de Costa Rica.

7. Son semejantes a una regla *(rule)*. Son esenciales para que funcione la sociedad.

Horizontal

2. Es la nacionalidad de un hombre de Venezuela.

3. Es un verbo que describe cuando una persona se va a vivir a otro país.

6. Es la nacionalidad de una persona de Ecuador.

8. Es la nacionalidad de un hombre del Paraguay.

9. Es un sustantivo para describir el estado de las personas que tienen muy poco dinero o recursos.

© Cengage Learning®

© 2016 Cengage Learning®. May not be scanned, copied or duplicated, or posted to a publicly accessible website, in whole or in part.

14.21 **Asociaciones** Find the word in the second column that is most closely related to the word in the first column.

1. _____ la guerra   **a.** español

2. _____ la riqueza   **b.** el refugiado

3. _____ hondureño   **c.** la paz

4. _____ el idioma   **d.** la pobreza

5. _____ el inmigrante   **e.** guatemalteco

14.22 **Ideas incompletas** Complete the following sentences with a word or expression from the vocabulary.

1. Un _____ es un acuerdo entre países para vender y comprar productos.

2. Las personas que nacen en un país son _____ de ese país.

3. En mi ciudad hay muchos _____ que vinieron para buscar trabajo.

4. A causa de los conflictos entre narcotraficantes *(drug traffickers)*, miles de _____

   cruzaron la frontera *(border)* para escapar de la violencia.

5. A diferencia de los Estados Unidos, en varios países hispanos es obligatorio _____

   en las elecciones presidenciales.

6. Médicos Sin Fronteras es un _____ que provee servicios médicos a las víctimas

   de catástrofes naturales y de conflictos armados.

Prueba tu gramática 3 y 4

Subjunctive with adverbial clauses and conjunctions

14.23 **Relaciones lógicas** Choose the logical adverbial expression to complete each sentence.

1. Viajaré a Chile (siempre y cuando / hasta / a menos de) tenga suficiente dinero.

2. Emigraré a España (a menos que / antes de que / a fin de) encuentre trabajo aquí.

3. La guerra terminó (aunque / como / en cuanto) se firmó un acuerdo entre los dos gobiernos.

4. Necesito trabajar más (a menos de que / con tal de / a fin de que) salir de la pobreza.

5. Necesitamos escribir cartas al editor del periódico (para / hasta que / en cuanto) protestar contra la nueva ley.

6. Voy a contratar a un abogado (tan pronto como / para que / en caso de que) nos ayude a emigrar.

14.24 **La inmigración** Complete the following statements with the appropriate form of the verb in parentheses.

1. Antes de que nuestros padres nos _____ (comprar) los boletos, debemos solicitar nuestros pasaportes.

2. Cuando uno _____ (tener) pasaporte puede hacer un viaje internacional, pero no puede inmigrar a otro país hasta _____ (recibir) una visa.

3. Después de que tú _____ (conseguir) la visa podrás mudarte a Uruguay.

4. Me mudaré a Barcelona tan pronto como _____ (poder) vender la casa.

5. Mis padres siempre hacen trabajo voluntario cuando _____ (tener) vacaciones.

6. El mundo no vivirá en paz sin que _____ (haber) diálogo entre las naciones.

14.25 **Aprendamos otro idioma** Combine each pair of sentences using the adverbial expression indicated. **¡OJO!** You will need to decide whether to use the subjunctive or not.

   Modelo   Conseguí un pasaporte. Viajaré a Sudamérica. (para)
   Conseguí un pasaporte para viajar a Sudamérica.

1. Quiero aprender español. Puedo usarlo en mi trabajo en el futuro. (para)

   _____

2. Es importante que todos hablen más de un idioma. Nos entenderemos mejor. (a fin de que)

   _____

3. Vas a estudiar todas las noches. Aprenderás todo el vocabulario. (con tal de)

   _____

4. Mi amiga y yo pensamos estudiar en España. Es demasiado *(too)* caro. (a menos que)

   _____

5. Julia y David siempre practican español. Visitan Miami. (cuando)

   _____

6. Es buena idea ser bilingüe. Hay clientes que no hablan inglés. (en caso de que)

   _____

14.26 **Oraciones incompletas** Complete these sentences logically. Pay attention to the use of the present indicative, present subjunctive, and infinitive.

1. La inmigración se acabará tan pronto como _____.

2. Los organismos internacionales hacen planes para que _____.

3. Yo emigraré cuando _____.

4. Los políticos discuten nuevas leyes de inmigración a fin de que _____.

5. La pobreza se eliminará después de que _____.

6. Mis padres siempre votan aunque _____.

Past perfect

14.27 **Un niño inmigrante** Rodrigo is a recent immigrant and this is part of his story. Complete the story using the past perfect.

Rodrigo tuvo que dejar su país cuando tenía seis años. Su padre (1.) _____ (perder) su trabajo

y su familia (2.) _____ (mudarse) a vivir con los abuelos de Rodrigo, en un pueblo pequeño

en la costa. Sus abuelos (3.) _____ (preparar) una habitación para Rodrigo, pero él extrañaba

su casa y a sus amigos. Un día, cuando Rodrigo llegó de la escuela, vio sobre la mesa una carta que

(4.) _____ (llegar) esa mañana. Esta carta les cambiaría la vida a todos. Dentro estaban las

visas que el papá de Rodrigo (5.) _____ (pedir) el año anterior. Aunque sus padres le

(6.) _____ (decir) que un día este momento llegaría, Rodrigo estaba sorprendido.

14.28 **¿Qué ocurrió primero?** Verónica is talking about her day. Using the information provided, tell what happened first. Be sure to use the past perfect and the word **ya,** as in the model.

Modelo   6:50 A.M.: El tren se fue.   6:55 A.M.: Llegué a la estación de trenes.
Cuando llegué a la estación de trenes *el tren ya se había ido.*

1. 4:00 P.M.: La reunión comenzó.   4:15 P.M.: Llegué a la sala de juntas.

   Cuando llegué a la sala de juntas _____.

2. 5:00 P.M.: Llegué a casa.   5:05 P.M.: Se fue la electricidad.

   Cuando se fue la electricidad _____.

3. 6:00 P.M.: El partido de fútbol comenzó.   6:15 P.M.: Encendimos la televisión.

   Cuando encendimos la televisión _____.

4. 8:00 P.M.: Terminé de ducharme.   8:01 P.M.: Alguien tocó *(knocked)* a la puerta.

   Cuando alguien tocó a la puerta _____.

5. 10:00 P.M.: Empezamos a cenar.   10:02 P.M.: Ocurrió un temblor *(tremor)*.

   Cuando ocurrió el temblor _____.

6. 11:00 P.M.: Me acosté.   11:10 P.M.: El teléfono sonó.

   Cuando el teléfono sonó _____.

14.29 Explicaciones There is a reason for everything! Using the phrases provided below, write complete sentences to explain each action or result. **¡OJO!** Remember to change the appropriate verb to the past perfect.

   Modelo los refugiados regresaron a su país / la guerra terminó
   Los refugiados regresaron a su país porque la guerra había terminado.

1. las personas regresaron a su país / terminó la dictadura

   _____

2. el expresidente de Colombia se mudó a Argentina / se casó con una mujer argentina

   _____

3. los ciudadanos celebraron / su partido ganó las elecciones

   _____

4. aumentó la pobreza / hubo una sequía *(drought)*

   _____

5. los planes para el tratado de comercio se cancelaron / los países se negaron a firmar el acuerdo

   _____

14.30 Mi vida Marcela is talking about some of the things she has done and what she had done previously. Write her statements using the phrases provided. Be sure to use the past perfect and the word **ya** as in the model.

   Modelo empezar la escuela primaria / aprender a leer
   Cuando empecé la escuela primaria ya había aprendido a leer.

1. conseguir la licencia de conducir / cumplir 16 años

   _____

2. graduarse de la escuela secundaria / decidir dónde estudiar

   _____

3. llegar a la universidad / encontrar una compañera de cuarto

   _____

4. ir a estudiar a Guatemala / estudiar español por tres años

   _____

5. terminar la universidad / recibir una oferta de trabajo

   _____

¡Hora de escuchar! 2

14.31 **¿Es lógico?** Decide if the statements you hear are logical (**lógico**) or illogical (**ilógico**).

1. lógico   ilógico

2. lógico   ilógico

3. lógico   ilógico

4. lógico   ilógico

14.32 **¿Lo había hecho?** Listen as different people talk about their beliefs and their experiences. Then choose the correct statement that applies to each situation.

1. a. Había vivido en otro país.   **b.** No había vivido en otro país.

2. a. Había estudiado otros idiomas.   **b.** No había estudiado otros idiomas.

3. a. Había votado antes.   **b.** No había votado antes.

4. a. Había recibido una beca.   **b.** No había recibido una beca.

5. a. La guerra había terminado.   **b.** La guerra no había terminado.

14.33 **La globalización** Listen to the information regarding globalization and decide which phrase best completes each statement according to the information provided.

1. Los teléfonos celulares y nuevas tecnologías en Internet han...
   a. creado una sociedad más impersonal.   **b.** facilitado la comunicación.

2. Los consumidores pueden encontrar...
   a. productos de mejor calidad.   **b.** precios más económicos.

3. La gente puede...
   a. viajar y conocer otras culturas.   **b.** buscar trabajo en otros países.

4. Un efecto negativo es...
   a. la pérdida de trabajos en algunos países.   **b.** la emigración de trabajadores a otros países.

¡Hora de reciclar! 2

14.34 El subjuntivo 1 Combine the elements to form logical sentences. Remember to use the present subjunctive and add the indirect object pronoun with the verb of emotion in addition to the word **que** between clauses.

Modelo los productores / preocupar / el canal / perder televidentes
A los productores les preocupa que el canal pierda televidentes.

1. los ciudadanos / no gustar / el congreso / querer anular la nueva ley

_____

2. los refugiados / alegrar / el gobierno / aceptarlos en el país

_____

3. el estudiante de español / interesar / el idioma / ser diferente del inglés

_____

4. la compañía internacional / molestar / el tratado de comercio / no permitirle aumentar sus precios

_____

5. los organismos internacionales / preocupar / la pobreza / seguir aumentando (*growing*)

_____

14.35 El subjuntivo 2 Complete the statements, using either the present subjunctive or the present indicative of the verb in parentheses.

1. No conozco a nadie que _____ (entender) esa ley.

2. Necesitamos un gobierno que _____ (poner) primero los intereses de los ciudadanos.

3. Tengo una beca que _____ (pagar) todos mis estudios.

4. Debemos proteger el derecho de votar que nosotros ya _____ (tener).

5. Queremos votar por un representante que _____ (escuchar) a la gente.

6. No hay ninguna organización internacional que no _____ (estar) interesado en los derechos humanos.

7. Buscamos una resolución que _____ (ser) aceptable para todos.

8. Conozco a varios inmigrantes que _____ (venir) de Latinoamérica.